Ready, Set,

RIPEN!

A Leader's Guide to **PREPARING PEOPLE** for **DEVELOPMENT**

Ready, Set,
RIPEN!

A Leader's Guide to *PREPARING* *PEOPLE* for *DEVELOPMENT*

SACHA LINDEKENS, PhD
and **JEFF GRADDY,** PhD

READY, SET, RIPEN!

A Leader's Guide to Preparing People for Development

Copyright© 2019 by

SACHA LINDEKENS, PhD
and
JEFF GRADDY, PhD

ISBN # 978-1-7327738-0-6

Published by:
Avion Consulting Publications
4142 Adams Avenue, Suite #103-532
San Diego, CA 92116
www.avionconsulting.com

ADVANCE PRAISE

Ready, Set, RIPEN! A Leader's Guide to Preparing People for Development is a compelling, useful and engaging book on mentorship and people development, aimed at coaches and organizational leaders. Having worked as consultant to leaders and leadership teams for many years, in the RIPEN model and the colorful stories of Rick and his colleagues at Karpos, I recognized the situations, and the shift in mindsets and behaviors that help individuals become effective coaches and mentors of their peers and teams. The book is written as a "business parable", which makes it an engaging read full of insights, actionable suggestions, and much food for thought. A great contribution by Jeff, Sacha, and their team.

JAIME MORALES, Partner, McKinsey & Company

I have had the fortune to work with both Sacha Lindekens and Jeff Graddy and witness their ability to work masterfully with leaders across industries. As psychologists they both have a deep understanding of what drives human behavior and know how to apply this to the practice of leadership development. This book addresses a key element often overlooked in leadership development: How to ensure leaders are ready and willing to change before providing them with tools or advice. Their book carefully walks practitioners, coaches, and managers through the many pitfalls and misconceptions of working with human change. It illustrates those beautifully with a compelling story all of us can relate to and provides highly practical tips. I can highly recommend this book to anyone who works with other people and whose job it is to facilitate successful change - that is everyone that works in business!

MATTHIAS BIRK Ph.D., VP of Leadership Development,
Pine Street, Goldman Sachs and Adjunct Professor for Leadership,
New York University

Masterfully written and wildly insightful, this outstanding book by Jeff and Sacha provides the perfect roadmap for how current and emerging leaders can propel growth and development in themselves and their teams.

BRENT GLEESON, Former Navy SEAL,
bestselling author of TakingPoint and CEO, TakingPoint Leadership

Sacha and Jeff have done it again! Their latest book creates a whole new approach to leadership coaching that is both relatable and actionable. Everyone will recognize themselves, colleagues and organizations in this book. This is a well thought out and engaging approach to presenting key skills needed to be a successful coach and change leader in today's rapidly changing business environment. The RIPEN model is a must-read for all leaders looking to up their game in generating long lasting behavior change in themselves and their team members.

BILL BRAND, Chief Retail Officer,
Carnival Corporation and PLC

As seasoned leadership experts, Dr.'s Sacha Lindekens and Jeff Graddy have brought the reality of coaching and talent development to life in their compelling fable. As a human resources professional, one of the challenges I face is identifying rigorous and practical talent development methodologies that business leaders will easily adopt. The RIPEN model strikes the right balance between theoretical rigor and real-world practicality. This methodology challenges many of the misconceptions business leaders have about how to coach and develop people, and is sure to benefit those leaders looking to further develop their talent development skills.

KATSUYOSHI SUGITA,
Head of HR, Microsoft Japan

TABLE OF CONTENTS

ACKNOWLEDGEMENTS

We want to thank the many people who contributed their time, wisdom and talent to this book. In particular, we want to acknowledge the critical role Sarah Ngu played with her expertise as a writer and storyteller, helping bring our experiences with clients to life. Sarah was a great partner who walked with us in lock step throughout the process. She is a very talented writer and we cannot thank her enough.

We are also grateful for Ehrich Johnson sharing his expertise in solar technology and the solar industry in general, without which we could not have woven such great reality into our story.

Much thanks go to our editor, Lauren Mix, and designer, Tamara Parsons, who are consummate professionals and a huge part of any success we find with this book.

We cannot give enough gratitude to our clients, without whom we would not be able to live out our passion of helping leaders unleash a better version of themselves, nor would we have all of the fascinating (and sometimes crazy) stories that made up the seeds of the names-have-been-changed-to-protect-the-innocent tale you are about to read.

We could not have been successful without the support and help of all of our colleagues at Avion Consulting. In particular, thanks go to

Christi Smith for her prowess in all things needing planning and execution, keeping us organized and on schedule.

And, finally, we have great love and appreciation for our families, whose love and support make it possible for us to do what we do. So, thank you, Laura, Taylor, and Reid, and Jenny, Ava, and Tyler. You support our obsession with helping our clients become better leaders and organizations, and stand with us as we try to help as many leaders as possible make work more meaningful and more productive. We appreciate your continued support for us even when we do crazy things – like writing our second book in two years.

INTRODUCTION

Like most experienced managers, executive coaches or HR professionals, you probably have found yourself trying to coach someone to make, what appears to you, a relatively simple change, only to find that he or she continues reverting to their old patterns of behavior. The micromanager who can't let go of the details of a project, the windbag who simply won't listen to another perspective, the tactically-oriented team member who won't elevate to focus on strategy, or the person who can't say no and is thus always behind in their deliverables are all examples of common challenges coaches try to rectify.

At first, most managers and coaches try to sell their coachees on merits of the behavior changes ("if you would delegate more, it would free you up for more senior level work and enable you to have better work-life balance"). To their surprise and frustration, this sound logic usually doesn't lead to long term behavior change, causing them to employ to a more "tell-oriented" style of coaching ("I want you to delegate this project to so-and-so by next week. You'll thank me later!"), which has a similar result. While the employee may indeed delegate that specific project, many find themselves unable to stay out of the details and revert to inserting themselves into the details of the project, much to the frustration of the team members or to you, the coach. Alternatively, the coachee may fully delegate that one specific project because the coach told him or her to do so, but there is no long lasting and systematic behavior change in the area of coaching.

In these situations, some leaders may move from the carrot to the stick and berate the individual publically or document the shortcoming on their year-end review. Other, more encouraging leaders may identify a mentor who is particularly strong in empowerment and encourage the individual to meet with them regularly. Yet, despite either tactic, the employee still does not make long lasting behavioral changes. Sound familiar?

In our experience, these well intended coaching strategies only work about 20% of the time. The other 80% of the time, leaders assume their employee isn't capable of such change and write them off as a failed effort, thinking that the person doesn't have the flexibility, skill or aptitude to learn the new behavior.

Increasing your coaching "batting average" above a 20% success rate is a competitive advantage for you and your organization. Great talent developers have a more productive and engaged workforce. They are able to retain talent longer and leverage their existing talent to be more effective.

It is extremely frustrating when someone you were unable to successfully coach makes the very changes you suggested through the coaching of a different leader. We want you to know that if you learn how to get people *Ripe For Development* you can flip the percentages and have meaningful impact in peoples' development closer to 80% of the time. As a rule of thumb, we think people are only truly uncoachable roughly 20% of the time. More often than not, it is the inability of the coach that is resulting in a low success rate. At the very least, we believe most coaches are far too ready to write someone off as uncoachable rather than examine their own skills in behavioral development.

Having both trained as psychologists and worked as executive coaches for many years, we have found that in order to effect long term change in someone, that individual must be "ripe" to change, which means open to and ready for it. The concept of "ripeness" was a critical commonality in determining success in thousands of coaching engagements, generating the greatest degree of long-term impact when present.

In some of the successful instances, the coachee was initially and innately eager to make the change for one reason or another. In others, the coachee was not initially ready to make a change, but ripened throughout the coaching process, eventually making long-term behavior changes. Regardless of the timeframe in which it took to effect a behavioral transformation, sustained behavior change did not occur until the individual was ripe for it.

This finding was further reinforced during the research we conducted for a book we wrote with Dr. John Gates, one of our partners at Avion Consulting, entitled *"How Leaders Improve: A Playbook for Leaders Who Want to Get Better Now."* In that book, we discussed the commonalities of leaders perceived as making the most significant improvements in their effectiveness, and how coaches, managers and Learning and Organizational Development professionals can leverage these insights in their efforts to develop others.

Sure enough, one of the most common findings from our interviews was our most improved leaders expressing their mental and emotional preparedness to make these changes. In *"How Leaders Improve,"* we identified the elements that determine how ripe someone is to make a specific change and, have subsequently developed an assessment and coaching methodology designed to enhance these elements.

Coaching is indeed a learnable skill, but some powerful and pervasive misconceptions need to be challenged if one wants to dramatically improve their coaching success rate. This book reflects our collective thinking about how to enable readiness for behavioral change. Our target audience for this book is managers looking to develop their team members, executive coaches looking to enhance their impact with clients, individuals looking to make meaningful, sustained performance improvements, and development professionals responsible for cultivating talent in their organizations.

To make our points more consumable and less theoretical, we have structured the book in the form of a business parable, with key takeaways and actionable tips combined with reflection questions at the conclusion of each chapter. Additionally, we offer an overall summary of the book's messages in its conclusion. We hope you can relate to Rick's challenges and enjoy his journey as a coach, and that, after reading this book, you ultimately find yourself more *ripe* for your own development areas and more skilled as a coach of others!

CHAPTER ONE

THE LIGHTBULB

"Strike!"

The catcher catches the ball and tosses it back to the pitcher. Rick Fisher watches his daughter, Joanna, scowl at the umpire, who merely shrugs back. At 5'11", Joanna is taller than most players and even umpires. She surveys the field with her bat perched casually on her shoulder and looks at the scoreboard, even though she already has the numbers memorized.

It's the bottom of the 9th inning. There is a runner on second base and the score is tied, 6-6. If Joanna gets this runner in, the Chasers win and advance to the playoffs, giving them a shot at the Spring Championship, for which all high school teams in their San Diego school district are vying. If she strikes out, the game will move into extra innings. The sun has already set and a cool, strong breeze is blowing through the stadium on this May evening.

Rick looks at his watch. He has a call with a new colleague, Ivan Naeman, in an hour at 8:30, which he is not looking forward to in the least. This was the agreement he made so he could leave the office early to catch Joanna's last game of the season (unless they make the playoffs), and it was no surprise that Ivan couldn't (or wouldn't) wait until tomorrow morning.

Ivan was hired several months ago to help turn around the company Rick works for, which makes solar panels, and he had not exactly endeared himself to Rick or others on the management team with his ultra-confident, know-it-all style.

Movement in the outfield interrupts Rick's thoughts. The outfielders are signaling each other to back up and a wide sea of grass is opening since Joanna hit two fly balls into deep center field in her last two at-bats. Joanna looks at Coach Erin who waves her over for a quick pow-wow. After a brief exchange, Joanna jogs back to home plate and glares at the pitcher.

Rick, holding his cell phone to record his daughter, starts biting his nails. He knows that Joanna hasn't homered at all this season and that she really wants to get one on her stats card, after coming so close the last two times. But she can't afford to fly out again. A simple hit, just over the heads of the infielders, is all that is necessary to end the game.

The pitcher winds up and releases a high, floating fastball – the exact type of pitch that Joanna loves to hit out of the park. Rick winces. Joanna lifts her left foot, curling her body inward before rapidly cutting through the air with her bat. Clink! The ball leaves Joanna's bat and arches over the pitcher's leaping glove before softly landing a few feet past second base. The center fielder is sprinting towards the ball, but she started too far back. By the time she catches up with it, the runner has rounded third base and is barreling home.

"Safe!"

Joanna lifts off her helmet and jumps up and down, running to her team who is sprinting out of the dugout. The crowd around Rick is standing up in cheers. Once Rick recovers from his surprise, he joins them.

After a riotous debrief the girls trickle out, and Rick hugs Joanna, congratulating her. "So did you mean to hit that line-drive or were you aiming for a home-run?" he asks.

"Dad!"

"What?"

"I can't believe you have so little faith in me. Of course I meant to," Joanna huffs and pulls out her phone. "Talk to Coach Erin. I gotta text Alexy."

Rick catches Erin's eye and walks over to her. He had admired her coaching style since she'd moved to San Diego from New York. Despite being new to the school, in a few months she quickly won the team's admiration and loyalty, which is something since the Chasers weren't exactly an easy crowd. They have plenty of ego to go around, especially Jo.

This season, under Erin, the Chasers were fourth in their league. Last season they placed 7th out of 10.

"I was sent by Jo to talk to you," Rick smiles, approaching Erin. "She claims she meant to land the ball there. Is that true? Congratulations by the way! Everyone must feel great."

"Yes, this means we have a shot at the championship next month," Erin responds, taking off her baseball hat. "And yes, I believe she intended to. She told me she was aiming to get it just over second base before she went up to bat."

"Are you serious? I've been telling her that all season: Stop swinging for the fences all the time. Bat smart. Get the runner in. But whenever I talk to her about batting strategy, it's like talking to a wall."

"Yeah, she is stubborn," Erin grins, watching Joanna's dirty blonde ponytail bob up and down, towering over everyone else. "When I first gave her feedback, she was really resistant."

"I know! She always says, 'But I'm a power-hitter, Dad!' So how in the world did you get her to listen?"

Erin turns to quickly wave goodbye to a family driving off in a mini-van, "See you next week Tan, Su Ann! Great diving catch, Lia!"

She turns back to Rick, smiling. "It's taken me almost nine months, but

I think I have every parent's name down now. I'm terrible with names. It is Rick, right?"

"Yes, people at work call me Fisher, but I don't care either way."

"Cool, Rick. So, first I made it clear that I wasn't trying to kill her super-power. I wanted her to keep being a power hitter, but also wanted her to adapt her style to the situation at hand."

"Was that it?"

One of Joanna's teammates came up to Erin and tapped her on the back. "Coach, now that we're in the playoffs, does this mean we'll have practice twice a week now?"

"Yes, Ashley." Erin turns to face her. "Weren't you there when I said we'll be practicing on Saturdays and Thursdays now? Or were you playing Angry Birds on your phone again?"

"Angry Birds is so last year, Coach," Ashley chuckles, rolling her eyes. She walks off, holding her phone up in the air. "Wait you guys, I think there's a rare Pokemon over by the bushes!"

"Apologies, you know how kids are these days," Erin says, turning back to Rick. "As I was saying, I think the real turning point was after the second game of the season. I overheard her talking to her teammates about how hitting home runs would catch the eye of college coaches. Once I heard that, I explained to her how college coaches think. An All-Star power-hitter on a team that rarely wins can be a red flag to them. They care if someone is a team player who wants to help the team win. Of course, it helped that I used to play college ball so I have some credibility."

"And that worked? We've been talking to a few Cal State coaches who have come out to see some of Jo's travel games."

"It took some time. But, once she understood that I just wanted her to better discern when and how to hit, she started listening more. Though, she really started taking notes when I reminded her that the chances of college scouts showing up at the Spring Championship game are much higher than at an average high school game, and that we aren't going to get there unless we, as a team, win."

"That's smart. Man, why didn't I think of that? I'm glad you were able to get through to her. I love her, but sometimes she really thinks she is God's gift to humankind."

Erin smiles. "I'm used to it. I grew up in a large family in New York City; the youngest girl with four older brothers who were all obsessed with baseball and thought they were God's gift to the sport. Ironically, I've stuck with sports a lot longer than they have."

"Oh yeah? I was an only child so I always wanted siblings, even with the fights and all, but let me tell you, I have more than enough ego to deal with now between Joanna and people at work,"

Rick replies. "That reminds me. I have a call in 30 minutes so I've got to start heading out. Oh, and there's Jo."

Joanna runs up and blurts out, "Dad, I need 15 more minutes." Before Rick could respond, Joanna is fading fast into the distance.

"Maybe I'll take my call here," Rick sighs. "You know, Erin, the issues you've been having with Joanna sound similar to those I've been having with this guy I have to call. Ivan is a talented All-Star, but he's not a team player and basically shuts down anytime I give him feedback."

Erin pauses and says, "Rick, why don't we walk and talk. I've got to make sure everything's cleaned up and put away."

"No problem," Rick says. They start walking towards the field, picking up discarded cans and pizza boxes lying around along the way.

"So tell me about Ivan."

"Where do I start? This guy is Mr.-Know-It-All. He's arrogant, rolls his eyes in meetings and says things like, 'That's not how we did it where I used to work,' which pisses everyone off. We're trying to hire a few analysts and he is only impressed by candidates with Ivy League degrees, because he's a 'Yalie,' as he would say."

Erin notices that Rick's face is getting red. She lets him finish then responds, "I'm familiar with the type. Before I moved to California, I was leading a division of a large pharmaceutical company in New York. There were plenty of "Ivans" and while they can be real assets, they can also be really challenging at times."

"Wow, I didn't know you had a business background. You're a real renaissance woman."

"Yeah, I retired early a few years ago and started coaching softball full time. Developing talent was always my favorite part of my job, and you might be surprised about the similarities between coaching employees and athletes. Can I ask why Ivan was hired if he is such a challenge?"

"Karpos is going through some major transitions, and, to be honest, we went with him because we wanted someone different from the usual Karpos-type," Rick answered. "Most of us are fairly down-to-earth, you know, traditional folks in blue jeans who would rather get on the phone than put on a suit and deliver some fancy PowerPoint presentation via video conference. Ivan really sticks out like a sore thumb and thinks it's beneath him to adjust even the slightest bit to the way we do things."

Erin flips through different sheets of paper with markings on them in a binder, and then looks up and asks, "Rick, what exactly does Karpos do?"

"We manufacture and install solar panels. We've been around for a couple of decades. Basically, we shifted our strategy six months ago and have decided to invest in servicing solar panels as well, not just selling them. This is the new business line, called Customer Experience, that Ivan came on to lead four months ago. It's a big shift for all of us, trying to be more full service-oriented as a company."

"Gotcha. Can you give me a hand with this?" Erin dumps a few softball bags into Rick's chest, almost knocking him off balance. He recovers and catches up with Erin as she heads out of the dugout. "What do you do at the company? And how do you interface with Ivan? Watch out for that mud hole," she points out as they walk onto the field.

"I'm VP of Sales. I've been with Karpos for five years now and I'm responsible for selling solar panels. Ivan is *supposed* to sell servicing of these panels to our customers, although he hasn't brought in any major deals yet. He's too busy "strategizing" with Bets, our CEO, in her office."

"So, do you have to work with him frequently?"

"We are technically working together on some of our major clients, but during our first few calls, he kept mocking new panel sales in front of clients, who didn't seem to enjoy his holier-than-thou attitude. So, lately I've been keeping a distance."

Erin reviews the field and dugout to ensure it is clean. "Headed to the parking lot?" she asks.

"Yes, I am. Although, I have to take my call first. But, uh, Coach? Have any pearls of wisdom on how I'm supposed to deal with this guy?"

Erin locks up a large bin, looks Rick in the eyes and asks, "Are you sure you want advice?"

"I do! I mean, I figure you may have some experience working with certain personalities, not that what happens on the field is what happens in offices of course, but—"

"No, I do think I have good advice to give. But I'm not sure you want it," Erin smiles.

Rick is a little stunned. "What do you mean?"

"First of all, do you believe in your company's decision to invest in servicing?"

Rick nods, "Yes, of course."

"And do you want Ivan to succeed in this new business line?" Erin starts walking, with several heavy bags strapped over her back. "I'm headed over there towards my car," she states.

"Ok, I can walk with you. I mean, it's not a question if I want Ivan to succeed. We don't have a choice. He has to."

Erin turns back to look at him. "Then why are you basically letting him sink or swim all by himself?"

Rick looks at her, startled. "I mean, I tried in the beginning…"

"You want my honest opinion, yes?"

"Of course."

"Ivan is not acting like a team-player, I agree, but it seems neither are you." Rick looks down at the ground. Erin sees Rick's reaction and softens her face. "Look, perhaps it's true that Ivan really isn't a fit with Karpos. But it doesn't sound like you have really tried to help him learn the ropes and give him a legitimate shot. You said it yourself that you've been keeping a distance lately."

She pauses to let Rick take in what she's saying before continuing, "Take Ivan out of the picture for a bit. How would you react if Joanna came to you and said, 'We have a new center-fielder and we all hate her personality. It makes us not want to play with her and, even though she is a good player, we hope she fails'?"

Rick considers this before answering, "Um, well, I would empathize but also be concerned because as a left-fielder, Jo has to work very closely with the center-fielder. I see where you are going here, Erin. I'd also tell her that the team winning is what's most important so she can't let personality issues get in the way unless they are truly egregious."

Erin gives Rick a knowing smile.

"But come on," Rick says. "You're making Ivan out to be some sort of saint, as if the problem is all on us."

"Alright then," Erin says, unlocking the trunk of her van. "Let Ivan fail. He'll get fired in a few months. Then you'll start the search process all over again. How long did it take to find someone for that role? Hang on. I've got to make some room to load this in," she says, rearranging its contents.

Rick hands her the softball bag he was carrying. He wipes his hand across his forehead even though he isn't really sweating. What Erin was saying was making him feel something he didn't like. He contemplated ending the conversation. He could see his daughter in the distance, looking for him.

Yet he knew that, even if he ended the conversation, Erin's words would still nag him. If he was honest with himself, he felt embarrassed criticizing Ivan for being a poor team player while he wasn't acting much like one either. And since he was being honest, he should admit that perhaps he was jealous of all the time Ivan spends in Bets's office and how Ivan is hailed by the board as the new golden boy who will save Karpos without them acknowledging all the years of labor that he and others had put into the company.

"The search process took a long time, yes," Rick finally replies. "And you're right. We can't afford to keep replacing people for this position. It's too critical. I'm willing to give Ivan a shot. Maybe he will change. But I've tried giving him feedback a few times and he just doesn't listen. Any ideas on what my next steps should be? After all, you got Jo to change."

"Ivan's not going to be an easy case, by any means, if what you've said is true. But maybe you and I have seen more stubborn people change their ways," Erin says as she locks her van and nods in Jo's direction. "Are you sure you actually want my advice in dealing with Ivan, as you asked earlier? I'm going to warn you: I try to be kind, but I give it to people straight."

"Well, Jo really does seem to have changed. Give me your wisdom, Yoda Erin," Rick teases as they walk back to the field.

Erin laughs. "Now this is going to sound very Yogi, but the truth is that I don't really need to say much more. Just reflect on what happened with Jo: If people aren't ready for change, they will not listen. So before you start giving them tips on *how* to change, start by understanding if they *want* to change. If they don't, focus on how to get them ready and willing. That's why I kept asking if you were sure you wanted advice. I needed to know you were willing to accept it before I continued. In my corporate career I found that's the first step in getting people ripe for change."

"Willingness?" Rick asks.

"Realization," Erin corrects. "People have to realize that something has to change, and that they are, at least partly, responsible for making that change. Basically, what you've just experienced. That feeling, I could see it in your eyes, it looked like a light bulb went off. "

"Yes," Rick says, embarrassed. "I realized that I was accusing Ivan of something that I was doing myself."

"That's what I call a 'light bulb moment'," Erin replies. "It's when the lights turn on and suddenly you see everything from a new perspective."

Right then, Joanna's voice booms across the parking lot. "Dad! Where are you? I've been texting you like crazy,"

"That's my signal," Rick says, turning to find his daughter.

"Have a good one, Rick. Thanks for helping me clean up. I will see you next week."

Rick turns around to locate Joanna's voice and finally notices that his pocket has been buzzing with notifications. He opens up his phone to see many emoji-filled text messages from Joanna and a voicemail from Ivan. A rush of anxiety hits him as he realizes that it's ten minutes after his call was supposed to start. He looks up and Erin is already gone.

TAKEAWAYS AND TIPS:

How do you get people to change? We've all been there, trying to get So-and-So to change their behavior for weeks, months or years, banging our heads against the wall while making no progress.

Maybe it's your nemesis at work ("Ivan" is quite a common scenario that our clients come to us with), maybe it's a direct report on your team who could be high potential if she would just tweak one aspect of her leadership style, or perhaps it's even your boss. The rest of the chapters in this book will explore Rick's relationships with Ivan and a handful of other colleagues in his workplace: Betsy, the CEO; Stephan, the Regional Director of Sales (one of his direct reports); and a couple of Millennial business analysts, Annie and Arthur. In each instance, Rick will have to figure out how to help his peers, his boss, and his direct report(s) become "ripe" for change—all in different ways.

This is not a book about change management as a whole, but rather about the first step of it; getting people ready and willing to change. Over the decades that we've been coaching individual leaders and executives, we've seen so many struggle to help their people get "ready and willing" to make a change that we came up with the RIPEN model to explain what needs to happen. RIPEN synthesizes our insights about the process people go through as they begin to consider behavior change and leadership improvement. RIPEN stands for Realization, Incentive, Pressure, Expectation and Natural Inclination.

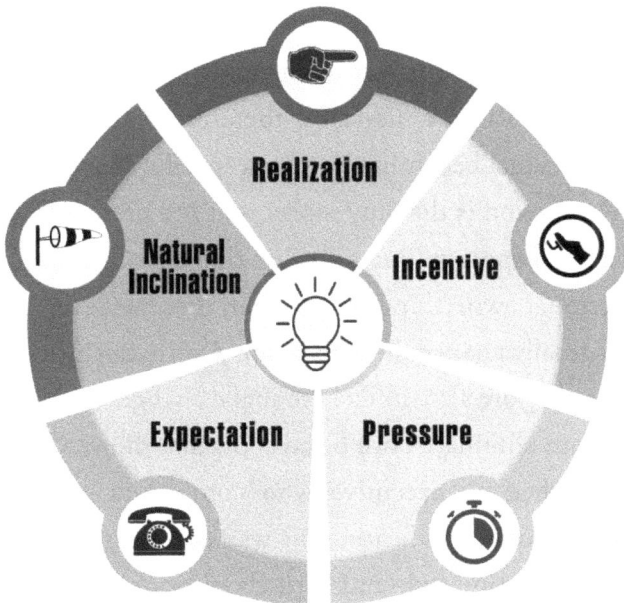

Each dimension of the model illuminates one of the key psychological dynamics involved in becoming open and willing to change. Simply expecting people to adopt advice without understanding the psychological dynamics at play is likely to be about as effective as Rick trying to coach his daughter to be a more strategic hitter or trying to influence his new colleague Ivan.

The first letter of the model is R, which stands for Realization. This is the first condition for ripeness. There are two parts to Realization: personal recognition that there is a need for change and personal accountability for making it. Both parts need to be operative for the Realization to have an impact.

Rick knew that the situation with Ivan was not sustainable, but he did not see himself as personally responsible, at least in part, for fixing it. He exclusively attributed the teamwork and stylistic issues as being the result of Ivan's lack of emotional intelligence, and saw himself and his Karpos colleagues as victims. Thus, the first condition for "ripeness" would not be met until he had his realization and both saw that his own behavior was hurting the company and recognized that he was responsible for this rather than blaming it all on Ivan. Once Rick assumed personal ownership for the need to change, he was on his way to changing his behavior.

As the acronym RIPEN indicates, there are many aspects that contribute to an individual becoming ripe for a specific change—the more the better—but Realization is the only aspect that is a prerequisite for change. If people have blind spots, failing to realize that a change needs to be made and assume personal ownership for making it, the chances are very, very low that they will actually change their behavior. Alternatively, if one assumes a victim mindset, they are also unlikely to make changes. Realization is what happens when you eliminate both blind spots *and* the victim mentality.

We once coached an executive who completely agreed with some feedback that she received indicating she was annoying her colleagues with her direct communication style and hard-charging approach. However, she also thought her colleagues were being overly sensitive rather than accepting responsibility to change her behaviors that were having a negative impact. Only once she both recognized their full impact *and* owned the fact that changing some behaviors was not completely her colleagues' responsibility was she able to make sustained changes that caused a positive difference with her colleagues (and her own goals).

There are many ways people come to their personal realization. Delivering feedback in a *penetrating* way is key. Many of the leaders we've worked with lack a basic understanding that a problem exists, so the delivery of pointed feedback can come as quite a shock to them. In this case, Erin's direct comment, "Ivan is not acting like a team-player, I agree, but neither, it seems, are you," woke Rick up to his need for change. Erin's feedback was penetrating, not because it was harsh or mean, although it was direct, but because it sparked cognitive dissonance for Rick, who clearly saw himself as a team player and judged Ivan for not being one. Erin was challenging Rick's victim mentality and promoting a sense of personal accountability.

Although Erin is not Rick's "formal" executive coach, that is the informal role she effectively plays throughout this book. Each coach has their own unique style; Erin's style is not meant to be a lesson for what coaches should do. However, there are general lessons to be learned from her *approach* for all coaches and leaders elaborated below. They are to empathize, ask questions and be direct when necessary while considering the other's perspective. To increase the likelihood of internalization, get the coachee to connect the dots and come to their own realizations.

IF YOUR COACHEE LACKS A HIGH LEVEL OF REALIZATION, BELOW IS A SERIES OF RECOMMENDATIONS.

- Ask as many open-ended, non-leading questions as possible in order to pose the opportunity in new ways. This also creates a better understanding of the context by challenging your own biases. It is critical that you see the problem or situation from their perspective, rather than forcing your judgement or interpretation of the situation on them – especially early in the process.

- Help them reflect on how the current issue fits into a broader pattern of behavior. We all suffer from behavior blind spots and it can be easier to "see" our impact when we step back and recognize that we are unconsciously acting consistently with how we often behave in similar situations.

- Collect 360° feedback and review prior performance evaluations with the individual to challenge blind spots. While you don't want to base your views exclusively on these, there are often long-standing behavioral patterns that will stand out over the years.

- Solicit feedback from other stakeholders. Get input from both advocates and adversaries – often, similar behavioral descriptions pop up (even though the interpretations of those behaviors may vary between those who are "fans" vs "detractors").

- Utilize valid, reliable personality assessments that focus on self-insight and personal development. We find that people will sometimes listen to independent assessments outlining their tendencies as much, if not more, than the 360° feedback they get from colleagues. Recognizing that underlying preferences can be drivers of their external behavioral patterns can be a strong motivator for some people.

- Ask your coachee what he or she believes his or her greatest strength is. Then inquire if there are any weaknesses or downsides associated with this strength. Development areas often go hand in glove with overused strengths, specifically in situations that are over-used or applied even in situations where they are not valuable.

- Consider the timing of your message. Is now the right time to encourage change? Some changes are more urgent than others (more detail on this in later chapters), so it is important to find the right time to ensure they can focus, learn, and grow from your coaching efforts. The speed of business is only accelerating and, as a general rule, people need to make change faster, not slower. However, there may be times where you raise the issue with your coachee, but agree to make the change when the time is right.

- Be clear about the facts. How many times has it happened? When and where is the behavior most problematic? In what instances is the behavior OK or even a positive (to contrast with the times when it's a problem)?

- Assess how direct your communication needs to be to promote self-awareness. For some people, a mild level of directness will be enough to promote awareness. However, other, more assertive/direct/confrontational individuals will appreciate and respect a direct "sledgehammer approach," provided they trust your intentions in delivering it. Bottom line: tailor the message to your coachee's typical level of directness. It should not be based on your own preferences around directness.

REFLECTION QUESTIONS

1. *Coaches perceived as credible have a leg up in influencing their coachees. What contributed to Erin's credibility as a coach to Joanna and Rick? What are the implications for you as a coach?*

2. *What was it that enabled Erin's message to penetrate, causing Rick to assume some enhanced level of personal account-*

ability for his workplace challenges? How can you construct your feedback messages to be similarly provocative?

3. *When Rick said "Give me your wisdom, Yoda Erin"? Erin responded by saying, "Now this is going to sound very Yogi, but the truth is that I don't really need to say much more." What was the impact of Erin's open-ended question? Why?*

4. *Giving advice on how to change will only be successful if the recipient of the advice acknowledges an issue needs changing. Have you ever given advice before knowing if the person was ready to hear it? What drives this behavior in you? How can you challenge it?*

5. *Do you have good self-awareness about your "default" coaching style? Most of us have a pattern of how we deal with coaching opportunities, but that approach may not work for everyone, every time. How can you discover your own coaching style? How do you identify situations that will likely require adapting your approach?*

CHAPTER TWO

THE BLAME GAME

For a company in a cutting-edge industry, Karpos's headquarters in San Diego is remarkably dull. Its building is tucked away in an industrial park with plain aesthetics, the inside not much better than the outside. The walls are gray with very few windows, spotted with various pictures of long-time employees and office softball games. Karpos occupies two floors in its building, with an assortment of cubicles and offices for executives.

CEO Betsy Trentanelli pays little attention to décor and aesthetic. "I'd rather look at graphs and spreadsheets than look at the walls," she quipped during an office tour with Rick on his first day, five years ago. However, Karpos's core values, carved in rectangular stones, hang prominently on the wall near the entrance: Humility, Teamwork, and Results.

Rick never gave those values much thought in his first few years at Karpos. Karpos is a friendly place where people don't take themselves too seriously or try to promote themselves a whole lot. Folks work hard for results, but also make time to joke around, gather for happy hour, and play softball games. The values blended into the background of Karpos and only started standing out to him about three years ago, when his wife, Melissa, died.

That year, Rick threw himself into his work to the point that others grew concerned. Lucinda, the VP of Marketing, offered to pick up Joanna from high school, as her son and Joanna were classmates. Tony, VP of Manufacturing, would come by at the end of the day, reminding him what time it was and asking if he wanted to go grab a bite or join the others at happy hour. Stephan, Regional Director of Sales, would drop by his office to casually shoot the breeze. Even Betsy would occasionally check in to see how he was doing.

Although he declined most of their offers, he felt grateful. He appreciated their concern and the fact that they respected his coping methods. They minded their business, gave him space and offered help occasionally. That's when Rick knew he wanted to be here for the long haul, that the "Karpos way" meant something real, like words carved into stone. That's why Ivan's personality really rubs Rick the wrong way. It just isn't the Karpos way.

❖ ❖ ❖ ❖ ❖

Rick is deep in concentration, flipping through a few resumes and interview notes as he closes the door to his office and sits down at his desk when the door suddenly swings back open.

"Rick! How's it going?" Ivan strides through.

"Hey, Ivan. I'm doing well. Are you settling into San Diego?"

Ivan smiles, "I've always thought of myself as a Bay Area person, born and raised, but knowing that I'm going to be here for awhile, I'm plunging into the local scene and getting involved with all sorts of stuff. I must say that I quite like San Diego. It's a nice change of pace."

Ivan quickly switches his direction. "Listen, glad we were able to connect last night. I gave Arthur and Annie a call. They start on Monday."

"Wait," Rick replies, frozen. "I thought we were still deciding who to hire to fill the business analyst role?"

"Well, I figured that since we liked both of them and really needed to fill that job *yesterday,* why not just hire them both? Besides, there's plenty of work to go around. We also have enough in the budget to hire both."

Ivan stands in front of Rick's desk, arms crossed with a slight smirk on his face. Ivan's perfectly pressed slacks and shiny sport-coat contrast Rick's plain khakis and collared shirt. Rick's face begins to redden as he rifles through the stack of papers on his desk.

"If they're starting Monday and today's Friday," he says, "that means they didn't give two weeks' notice to their current employer? Isn't that a bit unprofessional?"

Ivan raises his eyebrows. "Fish," he says, and then pauses. "You don't mind me calling you that, right? It seems like that's what people call you here."

"They say 'Fisher' not 'Fish.'"

"Right, Fisher," Ivan nods and starts pacing and gesturing, as if a professor giving a lecture in front of 300 freshmen. "You see, for Karpos to get to where we need to be, we have to pick up the pace around here. What was Facebook's motto? Move fast and break things. We must move away from the way things are usually done."

Rick interjects before Ivan can fully launch into his sermon. "I actually think Facebook changed that motto—"

"Doesn't matter," Ivan waves his hands. "Look, luckily we aren't public, but our investors are still looking for results. Data and machine learning are huge now in solar. There are startups popping up all over the place, analyzing customer data and using machine learning to predict those likely to buy solar panels. We're so behind that we need to hire these analysts immediately."

"I don't disagree, I am just wondering about the timing."

"Our investors want swift action. Weren't you on that call last week? It'll be huge to say that we've already acted and brought on a few data whizzes to help us increase the value we offer clients, better integrate Customer Experience and Sales, and be more strategic." Ivan claps his hands and waits, as if expecting applause.

"Keep in mind we were able to fend off that takeover last year. Our investors have our backs."

"Yes, but I hear from Bets that they've been questioning that decision and want to see greater ROI."

"Oh?" Rick wonders what else Bets and Ivan have been talking about. Ever since Ivan came on four months ago, they've been constantly huddling together. She used to swing by Rick's office first, but now her first stop is always Ivan's. Rick's stomach starts to react, but he pauses and remembers what Coach Erin said.

Rick hastily resumes his train of thought. "We have a 3 o'clock with Bets on sales strategy. I guess it's good that we have – what are their names again – Arthur and Annie onboard because they could help us out with some of the numbers."

"Great!" Ivan puts his hands in his pockets. "Glad we're on the same page. Besides, we shouldn't have to worry about performance—Arthur and Annie are young, but they have good pedigrees."

"Right, they're your type, Mr. Ivy League," Rick remarks.

"What do you mean by that?" Ivan's brow furrows.

"Just messing with ya. You know how we are here," Rick instantly regrets letting it slip out of his mouth. This is not the way he had envisioned confronting Ivan.

"No really, what do you mean? Do people have a problem with the fact that I have a degree from Yale and an MBA from UPenn? Because if so—"

Rick now can't help himself. "Actually, yes, sometimes people do."

"Would they prefer I went to community college then?"

"I'm not here to play your games, Ivan," Rick says, annoyed. "You know what I mean. It's not about your degrees. Sometimes people feel you are being condescending, that you're arrogant."

"I see. Should I now say that I went to college in Connecticut instead of at Yale?" Ivan chortles.

"No, it's not that." Rick feels more irritated. He hates it when Ivan does this. "It's when you say stuff like, 'At my old company we used to do it this way,' or when you make snide remarks about how Karpos moves at a snail's pace. It comes across like you are judging who we are as people because we don't have the same 'pedigree' or use the same fancy words. It feels like you aren't playing on the same team and, honestly, makes it harder for us to work with you."

Rick leans back in his chair, waiting for the light bulb to go off in Ivan's face. Any time now.

Ivan is calm. "I figured you would say that at some point. I've been sensing some tension in the air." He twirls his finger and continues. "But I can only be who I am. This is the way I've always been. I had no problems at SunDeck, Fithros or any other company. If people feel judged here, maybe they're just insecure. After all, didn't you hire me because you wanted some 'new blood'?"

"Yes, of course," Rick says, standing up, trying to even out the playing field. At 5'10", he stands a few inches below Ivan's six-foot frame. "I'm just giving you some friendly advice. You've got to start paying attention to how you come off to people and observe people's reactions to you."

Ivan shakes his head. "This is such petty stuff. We have much bigger things to worry about here at Karpos. People need to get over this."

"Well," Rick says as he reaches for his desk phone, "think about it. Not trying to say that I have all the answers or that I'm perfect. I just want to be candid and help you out. I've got to jump on a call in a minute though."

Ivan eyes him warily then slinks out the door. Rick watches him go then takes his hand off the phone. The call doesn't start for another ten minutes, but he wanted to get Ivan out of his office. Rick taps his notepad with a pen, trying to remember something. He suddenly puts down his pen and briskly walks out the door.

❖ ❖ ❖ ❖ ❖

"Stephan! Glad you are at your desk," Rick says.

Stephan Ford, the Regional Director of Sales, sits in his cubicle about twenty feet away from Rick's office. Dressed in well-polished brown shoes and a crisp, light blue shirt, Stephan is one of the top performers on Rick's team.

"I'm speaking with Lucinda from Marketing on our upcoming commercial campaign. I should have thought about inviting you earlier, but would you like to join the meeting? It'll be good for you to provide more insight into some of the strategic decisions we are making."

Stephan looks up, expectantly. "I'd be happy to, when is it?"

"It's in five minutes, unfortunately."

"Oh," Stephan winces. "I have a call in five minutes that I can't really move. Maybe I'll try to join at the end?"

Rick nods, "I'll see you later then." He turns back to his office, wondering what exactly it was that Stephan had a conflict with.

During the group-call with Marketing, Rick asks questions and jots down a few notes by hand on his notepad. He knows that eventually he'll have to type up these notes into an email to send to a few people, but this is the best way he can concentrate. Yet today, his mind continues wandering.

First, he thinks about how annoyed he is with Ivan and his grip on his pen gets tighter.

Why couldn't Ivan just *get it* the way Rick *got it* when Coach Erin talked to him? Shouldn't Ivan be grateful for Rick's feedback? After all, Rick didn't owe him that.

"The blue-blooded entitlement!" Rick thinks, as he shakes his head, drawing deep grooves of crisscrossed lines onto his notepad. Everything about Ivan is oppositional to the Karpos values of Humility and Teamwork. The only reason he was hired was that it was thought he could get Results, the third value. Someone on the call says Rick's name over the phone, jolting him back to the call.

When the conversation moves away from him, Rick's mind once again drifts, this time towards Stephan. He likes Stephan. Who doesn't like Stephan? He's hard working, consistent, a team player, technically savvy, and great at closing deals. He could see him taking over his job as VP of Sales one day, which is why he promoted him to oversee the Southwest (Karpos's biggest region) a few months ago. This was Stephan's time to show that he could manage at a more senior level and prove to Rick and the rest of the executive team that Rick had made the right call in identifying Stephan as his successor. Rick did have a few areas of concern with Stephan, in particular his micromanagement of his team, but the Southwest team had been consistently hitting their numbers ever since Stephan took it over.

Shortly after the call ends, Stephan pops his head into Rick's office and asks, "Is it over?"

"Yes, we just hung up. Don't worry about it. Have you had lunch? No? Let's get something to eat. It's a quarter to noon."

As they walk to their go-to food truck ten blocks away, Rick tells Stephan, "You know that Ivan and I have been deciding between two candidates to hire for the analyst position, right? It's Anna and Archie, or wait, Amy and Andy? I always get their names wrong. They're young, midtwenties. Ivan decided to the pull the trigger without really telling me and they're starting on Monday. They'll be helping Ivan and me with data stuff. You'll probably work with them at some point too."

"Sounds just like Ivan to bulldoze ahead like that. But actually, I already know about this. Ivan bumped into me in the hallway and told me,"

Stephan says. "I told him that I'd be happy to give them an intro to the Southwest region. And it's *Annie* and *Arthur.*"

"Figured you would already be on top of it," Rick smiles. "What was the big call you had at 1pm? Did the President of the United States call?"

"Yes, the White House wants every federal building to go solar by 2020 and they want our help," Stephan laughs. "No, I was talking to Calcyde."

"Calcyde…"

"They're a wholesale distributor in California. We're talking about partnering."

"Of course, I know them. That wasn't my question—"

"Next!" Stephan and Rick realize that they've been holding up the line for a few seconds. They walk up to order.

"So, as I was saying, Calcyde is a big distributor so it would be great if we could partner with them," Stephen continues.

"That's Jamie's account, right?"

"It is Jamie's, yes," Stephan says as he takes some napkins from a cup on the table. "Don't worry, I'm just helping. When I heard Jamie got this lead, given the size of Calcyde, I asked him if he needed help. He was glad that I offered, as he is swamped this week. It's no big deal, Fisher."

"Was Jamie on the call with you?" Rick asks, starting to feel a bit concerned.

"He was."

"And, how was he?"

"He was fine. Don't you want to know how Calcyde responded?"

Rick sighs. "Of course I do, but just remember that article I sent you from HBR or somewhere: Your job now has to be 20 percent direct sales, 80 percent helping people with sales."

"Yes, I've read that and plenty others that you've sent me on 'micromanaging.' I know I have to let go. I did try to let Jamie take the lead on the call."

"Ok, that's great. So, just to double check here, if Calcyde has a question tomorrow, would they call you or Jamie?"

Stephan pauses a little too long before he says, "Jamie."

"That's good. I hope it pans out," Rick says. The guy in the food truck calls their numbers and Rick jumps up to pick up their food. Their conversation gradually lightens from the next steps with Calcyde and solar pool heating systems to the Padres versus the Dodgers and summer vacation plans.

❖ ❖ ❖ ❖ ❖

Meanwhile, back at the office, Bets is prepping for a quick meeting with her Executive team. She just got off the phone with a board member, who was trying to get Karpos to move their manufacturing plants from Vietnam to the U.S. given recent tariff changes. It wasn't a bad idea, but, given the pressure Karpos has been receiving from investors to increase profits in the short term, an investment in plant re-location would take too long to pay off. Betsy felt slightly annoyed by the board members' presumption that she hadn't already thought of this idea and run through the calculations, but she was used to people underestimating her.

"You would think," she muses to herself, "that starting a company in a fledgling industry, under attack by utility heavy-weights, and growing it for over two decades would be proof enough to people of my resourcefulness."

Her mind switches to the investor call coming up at the end of the quarter. They need to have data to support launching the service division of their business. She likes the strategy that Ivan's drawn up thus far: Offering cleaning, upgrading and maintenance services for residential and commercial panels, as well as providing technical training, support and policy consultation to distributors and providers. Given the growth of solar over the past decade, this new business unit could realistically double Karpos's EBITDA over the next five to seven years.

However, Ivan and Rick aren't collaborating effectively, which, she believes, is reducing their ability to deploy the strategy and cross sell effectively. She wonders if she should raise the issue, but decides against it since they're adults and she's got bigger fish to fry. She walks into the conference room, adjusting her glasses and bun while gripping her laptop with one hand.

❖ ❖ ❖ ❖ ❖

It's 2:59pm, and Betsy is watching the clock, ready to begin. The last few people make it to their seats just as the clock changes to 3:00pm.

"Okay team! We have many things going on, but I want us to focus on two things before the weekend hits. First, I want to understand the significance of the dip in poly sales over the last few quarters. What's going on there? I'd like more insights. Is this an industry dip, as I've been hearing? What's the six-month forecast?"

Ivan and Rick both try to speak first, but Ivan races ahead, "Good news, I – Fish and I – have made the decision to bring on two analysts who will help us dive deeper into the analytics. They're starting Monday and I will get them started on that report."

"Good. Tell the analysts that I'd like something back to me by end of next week. Moving on," Betsy barely glances above her laptop as she continues.

"But wait," Ivan interrupts. "What are we going to do in response to the tariffs? I see SunDeck has already sent out a press release stating they are hiring more locally and looking to bring manufacturing back to America. Their entire website has the word 'America' plastered all over it: Made in America, America first. It's been weeks and we haven't said anything or responded in anyway."

"We have no idea if 'hiring more locally' means they'll hire one more person or have an additional plant, so let's not assume," Lucinda Bayfield,

VP of Marketing, calmly responds, with a slight edge to her voice. "And the moves of a single company, no matter how highly you regard them, should not dictate our marketing plans."

"I'm just saying that not many people understand the nuances of solar technology, but they do understand the difference between 'Made in America' and 'Made in Vietnam,' and I want us to be able to compete out there," Ivan says.

Tony Ahmad, VP of Engineering, who has been listening with furrowed brows and arms crossed, decides to speak up, "Ivan, you seem to think that manufacturing is just as easy as picking up our plants in Vietnam and dropping them in Texas. Do you have any idea what—"

Betsy brings the conversation to a halt. "Ivan, you're not alone in your concerns. I've been getting a lot of heat from some board members about tariffs, to be honest." She pauses for a slight moment and continues. "But I've worked out the numbers with Finance and it doesn't make sense to make any drastic manufacturing changes. I want to stick to the agenda for today. Luce?"

"Right," Lucinda clears her throat. "As you all hopefully know, the Arizona Supreme Court ruled recently that homeowners who lease rooftop solar panels will receive breaks on their property taxes. That was a huge win for solar! Now our industry is definitely in the headlines of local newspapers as well as the Wall Street Journal, not to mention that solar is still growing in both residential *and* commercial, *despite* new tariffs. So, Bets and I talked and we want to do a big marketing campaign in Arizona. We're thinking of emphasizing how we really own the solar process from end-to-end – 'from manufacturing to sales to services. We take care of all your needs.'"

Rick turns to her and says, "Luce, I like the idea. One of our biggest and oldest clients, Ten Zero, is a large real-estate developer based in Tucson and has huge name-recognition in that state. We could explore partnering with them on some marketing efforts."

Betsy chimes in, "Loved your work on this thus far, Luce. Fisher, am I right to believe you have something coming up with Ten Zero at the end of June?"

Rick is always surprised at how sharp Betsy's memory is. He hastily replies, "Yes, that's more than a month away, but we're preparing. Ivan and I have a meeting scheduled with them to talk about servicing panels. They may be looking to upgrade their panels as well, so we'll be discussing that too. Best case scenario, we could be looking at $5 million."

"That's fantastic," she replies. "That meeting is very important. We have an investor call the following week. If we can say that we've signed up Ten Zero to purchase our new panels with a 10-year servicing contract that would be huge in securing our investors' trust. Lining up these big contracts would play very well into our Arizona marketing campaign too.

"I don't want us to wait on them though. Let's be proactive and close that before the end of the second quarter. Fisher, remember when we lost that Argan deal last year because Sun Deck out-hustled us. Can't let that happen again."

"Yes, I remember." Rick looks down on his notes, wondering why Betsy always has to remind him that he dropped the ball on their biggest potential contract last year.

"And you and Ivan need to work together to start putting some results on the board," she says, making eye contact with them both. "Remember, we work as a team. It's the Karpos way."

Ivan and Rick do not look at her or each other.

She then pulls up her calendar on her laptop. "I believe I'll see Todd at a fundraiser next week, so I'll try to get a sense of how they are approaching their energy strategy. Last I heard, he was still leading operations at Ten Zero, although that job seems to be a revolving door so who knows how long he'll last."

"Bets, to circle back," Rick starts, "what kind of campaign do you want to push in Arizona? General education or product? TV? Billboards? Given the demographics there, we've had mixed results with our social media effort. What are you thinking?"

"I think that's your job to figure out," Betsy states without blinking. "Who's next in terms of updates?"

"I'll go next," Ivan replies. "I must say that I've been on calls with some of our key account managers and feel they still operate in a very transactional way. They – and all of us, to be honest – need to shift mindsets to think more in terms of building relationships for the long haul and understanding all the solar needs of our customers, from financing to maintenance to policy guidance rather than just closing individual sales. We need to think about the lifetime value of the customer and net promoter scores."

Betsy asks, "Did we change up the performance metrics for account managers yet?"

Rick responds, "Not yet. Ivan and I are still in the midst of working that out."

Betsy looks agitated and says, "It's been four months since we started talking about this and every time I ask, it's the same answer. What is going on?"

Rick tries to respond, but she cuts him off.

"I understand you're juggling a lot of things, but this is on you since most of the account managers still report to you. Talk to me when it's done."

Rick nods fervently, trying not to break off eye contact. He knows that she views that as a sign of weakness. He also knows he's been behind on this project, but there *are* so many other priority items he's juggling so her tirade was a bit uncalled for. Yet recently, not a week goes by without a blow-up of sorts from Betsy. Each quarter, profits are dropping – although the company is still very profitable – and the pressure is climbing.

As the meeting closes, Ivan follows Betsy out the door to pitch his latest idea to her; partnering with credit unions to offer solar financing. Rick watches them go and releases a deep exhale.

Nowadays, meetings with Betsy usually end with a new stack of to-do items and super high expectations, occasionally topped with a reminder of his latest failures. She is whip-smart and he respects her immensely – starting a company is no easy endeavor, especially in the volatile solar industry – but sometimes he wishes that she could be…. He didn't exactly know.

He joined Karpos five years ago because he was impressed with what Betsy built over the past two decades from the ground-up. Her family was in the energy business already, but she was the only one who saw solar coming over the horizon and jumped on it. From day one, she's run Karpos with a tight fist, but with a soft touch as well. Her sharp memory means that she will never forget any mistake you've made or what you've promised to do, but it also means that she remembers birthdays and other important personal details of her employees. During his first few weeks at Karpos Rick recalls being impressed that Betsy asked him how Jo was handling the transition to middle school. It was a small detail that somehow came up during the interviewing process, yet Betsy had remembered.

However, the past few years hadn't been easy for Betsy and Karpos as a whole. They had struggled with both the ability to scale quickly enough when the government subsidies were offered, and adapting to various regulatory and policy changes. They lost market share to bigger solar players, fended off hostile takeovers, and competed with innovative startups with sexier, smarter products. Betsy responded by running Karpos with an even tighter fist and the softer touch that brought Rick over to Karpos slowly faded.

❖ ❖ ❖ ❖ ❖

Rick drops by Stephan's cubicle on his way to the men's room.

"You look wound up, Fisher," Stephan says. "Fish tacos didn't go down well?"

"Yeah, well," Rick doesn't register Stephan's joke. "We're launching a big marketing campaign in Arizona. I know you just took over that area, but I need you to work with Marketing on that campaign. Make sure we're segmenting customers appropriately and all."

Stephan nods, "Sure, I'll check in with Lucinda."

"Also, Bets mentioned a dip in poly sales in the past few quarters. I looked at our dashboard and it looks like it's mostly coming from the Southwest. What's going on there?"

"Um, I'll find out and get back to you."

"Great. One other thing; the meeting with Ten Zero—I know you brought that account in—let's be proactive on that. Bets doesn't want Sun Deck or some upstart to steal them from us under our watch. And one more thing, why haven't we closed with FreshCo, that huge grocery chain in Arizona yet? I thought everything was supposed to be signed by this week. We've got to close that deal to make this month's numbers. What's going on?"

"The last I heard Nytasha said that they were reviewing the contract by today. It should be wrapped up in a few days."

"*A few days* is too vague," Rick is shaking his head. "It must be done by April 30th."

Stephan watches Rick walk back into his office. He hates that Rick has a habit of saying "one more thing" when in reality it was always more like three. Still, Stephan realizes that Rick took a chance by promoting him to this position over others who have been here longer. He's grateful for that. And now Stephan feels like he has to work twice as hard as anyone else to prove that he deserves it. Already, he's been hearing whispers of "affirmative action" regarding his promotion. Karpos is somewhat diverse, but he is one of the few black men on the sales team. And he's dead set on proving his critics wrong.

❖ ❖ ❖ ❖ ❖

Later that evening, when Rick arrives home he cracks open a beer and starts preparing the grill. Ever since Melissa passed, he's worked to improve his cooking. His doctor has been telling him to eat healthier as well, which is why he's trying to eat more fish, a drastic shift for someone who grew up on meat-lover's pizza and burgers most nights of the week.

The door opens, and Joanna waltzes in with her backpack. "Dad, veggie burgers *again* for dinner?"

"They are good for you."

"Mom would never believe this. She was always on you about eating vegetables. I can't believe now I have to beg you to cook a real burger once in a while."

"Well, you can go out tomorrow with your friends after practice for burgers and shakes if you want."

"I can't. I'm carpooling with Erica and she's gluten- and lactose-free so there's no way her parents would drop us there," Jo explains.

"Oh," Rick looks up from the grill. "What if I drive you this time? Coach Erin will be there, right?"

"OMG, Dad! Don't tell me you have a crush on her."

"Don't be silly, Jo," Rick says as he flips over a few burgers. "I just want to ask her some questions about work. She seems to have worked a miracle on you and the Chasers—"

"I know! We're going to be in the playoffs! I love Coach Erin," she exclaims. "We all love her. But she's working us hard. Now we have practice like a gajillion times a week."

"Okay well, I'll drive you to the practice tomorrow at 10:30," he states.

❖ ❖ ❖ ❖ ❖

The next morning, after letting Joanna out of the car, Rick parks his car and finds a sheltered bench nearby the batting cages while he flips through his Stephen King novel, occasionally checking stats from his MLB app.

"Rick, I don't usually see you out here on Saturdays," Erin spots him and waves.

Rick walks over and makes small talk, chatting about Joanna's progress and the team's recent victory over the second-ranked Titans.

"Hey, do you remember what you told me on Tuesday?" Rick abruptly changes the subject. Erin nods. He goes on, "Well it's not working. Ivan barely blinked when I gave him feedback that he's not a team player. I tried to get him to realize the impact of his behavior on the team, like you did to me, but I couldn't get through to him. And I tried to do the same thing with this guy, Stephan, who reports to me. I've talked to him multiple times now about not micromanaging and nothing has improved. I'm beginning to worry that maybe I made the wrong call and he's not ready to manage. I feel like I've been hitting a wall. So, my question is, do you feel that sometimes there are people who just aren't ever going to change?"

"You know, when I first started coaching, I used to think that 80% of the players on a team were set in their ways and never going to change so I focused on the 'coachable' 20%. But I learned that the numbers are actually flipped. Typically, 80% of players or team members can and do want to change. It's just about figuring out how to get them ripe for it. The rest of the 20%, well, that's another conversation," laughs Erin. She offers Rick some sunflower seeds, but he declines. She continues, "What exactly did you say and what was his response?"

"I told him he came off as somewhat condescending and elitist. I tried to be direct. And he basically said, 'This is who I am, I've always been this way and I've never gotten any feedback about this. The problem is you guys.' He refuses to take any responsibility. It was irritating."

"So," Erin says, chewing the seeds. "Good effort, first of all. I know it wasn't easy for you to do that. But let me ask you this, if Ivan decides tomorrow to give you feedback and you feel like he is asking you to make a fundamental change to your personality, how would you react?"

"Psh," Rick scoffs. "That was not what I said to him. I just said that he came off as judgy and condescending…"

"No, my question was not how would you react if that's what he said, but how would you react if that's how you *felt* about what he said."

"Well, to be honest, I'd probably wonder what gives him the right to tell me anything. I mean, he's the new guy, who isn't fitting in very well. But I wouldn't say that."

"Yes," Erin laughs, folding her arms. "I can see where Joanna gets it from. I believe she said something similar to me in the early days when I was trying to get her to improve batting."

Rick leans in, "Oh yeah? What did she say?"

"The predictable stuff. 'Who are you to tell me how to hit, you've just joined our team, everyone knows I'm a power hitter,' that type of thing," Erin replies.

Rick laughs, "I'm embarrassed she said that to you, but that's my girl. That's Jo, for better or worse. Alright, I see what you're saying."

"Yes, so put yourself in Ivan's shoes. What might he have been thinking?"

"Well, first he's probably thinking about whether his slacks were ironed correctly this morning," Rick jokes. "The second thing that might pop into his head is, 'Why is Rick suddenly giving me advice? Why should I trust him when we've been squabbling this whole time? Plus, why is this guy blaming me for problems I didn't create?'"

"I don't know Ivan, but based on what you said, that is likely the case. So, you've got to start earning his trust. You've been telling him that he's not a team player, but you should ask yourself how you have tried to show that you are on his team."

Rick silently nods, staring into the distance. "This is getting to be a little bit more complicated than I bargained for," he thinks.

"The next time you bring this up, try to emphasize that you are not really asking him to overhaul his entire self—"

"Although, that would be nice," Rick smirks.

"Yes, but you're not his priest," Erin smiles. "I grew up Catholic, pardon my jokes. When it comes to work, you're going to have a lot higher coaching success rate when you ask others to tweak their behavioral style, not change their core." She spits out another seed. "And if you can, avoid telling him what he needs to realize. Ask questions so he can get there by himself, like I did with you."

"This is a lot to remember," Rick scratches his head and adjusts his baseball cap. "This coaching stuff is hard. I don't know how you do it. I'd rather not deal with it, but the boss has been giving me and Ivan the eye. I think she knows something's up. What about Stephan? How do I know if I made the right call in promoting him?"

"I don't know much about Stephan, and I've got to go now, but I'll leave you with this," Erin turns to face him squarely. "It sounds like he's gotten the message from you several times. You guys have a good relationship where he trusts you, right?"

"Yes, we get lunch all the time."

"Ok, then think about incentives. Let's say someone knows they have to change. That's the first step. But what incentive do they have to actually do so? That's the next step. Think about incentives like the gas pedal in a car. It doesn't matter if you have a great car, if you don't have the gas pedal to get it moving it's just a big pile of metal."

"So you're saying," Rick thinks carefully, "that I should think about what will get Stephan motivated to change, to move him forward, so to speak?"

"Yes," she replies, "but incentives can be a bit more complicated than that. Most people aren't stupid. They usually do whatever they are doing for a reason. Sometimes that reason is outdated and no longer valid, but it still feels real to them. Joanna had her reasons for changing her batting strategy – she wanted that scholarship."

Rick nods slowly. "It's like we were revving her engine with the parking brake on."

"Yes," Erin smiles. "So first, lift the brakes *then* hit the gas pedal. Think about what incentive Stephan has to keep doing whatever he is doing now, and alternatively, what incentive he has to change his management style."

Rick folds his arms across his chest. "I would think that the incentives to change are clear for both, but maybe I haven't been clear. I'm not sure what incentive he has for continuing to micromanage. I've never really thought about that. Thanks for your advice as always. And look, if there's anything I can do to help you with the team, just let me know!"

Erin smiles. "Keep being patient with your colleagues. When they're ready to hear your feedback, they'll be glad you are there to help. As someone used to say to me, *when the student is ready, the teacher will appear.*"

☑ TAKEAWAYS AND TIPS:

Rick is someone who gets excited about something told to him, grasping a kernel of truth, and immediately starts teaching and telling everyone before fully internalizing the lesson. One of the mistakes he made, common of many managers coaching their team members, is that he assumed what worked for him would work for others. He came to his realization pretty quickly, but he assumed that everyone's journey would look like his—some direct feedback, the proverbial "light bulb" going off, and voila. If only!

As Erin mentioned, most people don't like to be told they should change who they are or compromise their identity. They build up defenses, like psychological calluses, to avoid hearing difficult truths about themselves. When we deliver 360° feedback to our coaching clients we often hear some version of, "I can point to a number of instances that are contrary to that feedback," "That person is biased so their feedback doesn't really hold water," or, "Are you asking me to change who I am?" Almost all of these reactions are defense mechanisms against information that doesn't line up with their reality. Therefore, a direct "attack" isn't always the most effective.

Framing things in terms of *behavioral* change, rather than *core* change is more effective. We should be asking, "What would be a better behavior for you to choose given this specific context?" rather than, "How can you change yourself?"

Ivan's defensive rationale that his style worked at previous companies is common as well. There is not "one best" leadership style for all situations so Ivan's style may very well have worked in previous contexts, but the point is that it's not working currently. Additionally, we can't be sure that Ivan never received any negative feedback about his style in past contexts. Maybe he did receive it, but chose to ignore it or trivialize it as well. That's why, when we work with new hires, we sometimes request 360° reviews from their *former* colleagues too.

Helping people get past the "blame game" is the first step to productive behavioral change. People, often unconsciously, tend to reject feedback that is inconsistent with their self-identity. Thus, Ivan may well believe that his style worked perfectly well in previous companies, despite indirect feedback suggesting otherwise. We see this frequently and to create penetrating messages and self-awareness, need to identify patterns of behavior or solicit input from multiple stakeholders.

To facilitate a shift in perspective from blaming others or the context to personal accountability, focus attention on the current reality (or future reality, if things are changing rapidly) and what can actually be controlled. When someone says, "I have never heard this feedback before! This style worked in my last company," we might respond with, "Well, you are hearing it now and it's not working here!"

Who bears the message of change also makes a difference. Rick, being his boss, could be direct in his coaching with Stephan. But with Ivan, a peer, he is usually – although not always – better off taking a more indirect, facilitative approach, asking Ivan questions to come to his own realization.

The correct question to ask is how direct a message needs to be in order for the recipient to hear it. Often times the answer is based on the recipient's personality not their role within the company. It is best to begin at a moderate level of directness and adjust accordingly. Too often, feedback providers default to their own directness comfort zone, rather than determining what level of directness will be most familiar to the recipient.

Getting others to change requires stepping outside of oneself and trying to understand the world through their eyes. Great coaches are particularly effective at asking their coachees questions that enable them to take accurate stock of their strengths and development areas, and also identify their own compelling reasons to make change. Realizations need to make sense in the coachee's language. Listening is so important, in part because it tells you how to position a message for maximum impact.

Invest continuously in people's development. Change doesn't typically happen overnight. Stephan and Ivan didn't "get it" with one conversation. Rick has to work and invest in understanding what motivates both of them and what does not, what language they use, what habits they have, etc.

I for Incentive, the next letter in the model, will be introduced in greater detail in the next chapter. Behavior change is hard and Rick must have an incentive to change his behavior, as must Ivan and Stephan. Some incentives are external to oneself (promotion, bonus), whereas some incentives are internal (personal values like the desire to be a team player, improve, or be successful). In Rick's case, both internal incentives (values around being a team player) and external incentives (a desire to meet his numbers and get a full bonus) are at play. Coach Erin helped Rick connect the dots between Ivan's success and Karpos's success, which impacts Rick's individual success. Rick also strongly values cooperation and collaboration, and thus is internally motivated to live consistently within these.

IF YOUR COACHEE IS NOT TAKING SUFFICIENT OWNERSHIP OR ACCOUNTABILITY TO HAVE A HIGH LEVEL OF REALIZATION, BELOW ARE A SERIES OF RECOMMENDATIONS FOR YOU TO CONSIDER.

- When your coachee presents you with a challenging situation and blames others for the difficulty, challenge their passive victim mindset by focusing on how they caused or exacerbated the situation, not on what others contributed to it. Emphasize that, although external factors may contribute to a situation, we cannot expect other people (or uncontrollable market forces) to change, so find ways to improve the situation yourself.

- Encourage your coachee to stop using "loaded" language to talk about an issue. Replace words like *blame* or *fault* with neutral words like *responsibility* or *accountability*. Also, substitute extreme descriptors and absolutes *(always, never, nonstop)* with more accurate and realistic phrasing *(often, usually, regularly)*. The words people use matter, as they shape their emotions and their mindset. Using negative and loaded language does not help them "realize" their part in making the needed change.

- If a coachee continuously blames others and focuses on what others are doing (or not doing), have them create a visual representation of responsibility – a literal "pie chart of blame" – so they can see that, while circumstance and other people may be partially to blame for their difficulties, they have to own their "slice of the pie" as well!

- Describe the person's behavior as if you were talking about a third party then ask them for coaching advice as if they were coaching that "mystery" person.

- Focus on the implications or consequences of their behavior. Try presenting their view of the situation (that the consequences aren't really their fault) coupled with your view (that their behavior in some way leads to or contributes to these consequences).

- Focus on describing the unintended outcomes they are creating. Often people focus on their ***intent*** or what they want to be true, and they avoid (or don't realize) the fact that there are ***unintentional consequences*** too.

- Trust matters a great deal in terms of coachees being receptive to tough feedback. Be sure to articulate your intention for delivering the feedback. This often sounds like, "My goal is to help you be an even more successful leader. You may not like or agree with my message, but know at the outset, that this is my intention." While the message may still be challenged, the coach rarely, if ever, is perceived to be attacking the coachee when using this approach.

- When discussing a behavior, proactively highlight what you believe the coachee's intentions are as well as indicating how they likely perceive their impact. Once accurate empathy is demonstrated, you can pivot to another perspective and begin showing them how their behavior is impacting others.

For example, if coaching Bets on her sharp-elbowed style, we would highlight how she cares about people and is a direct and results oriented leader who wants everyone to be successful together (thereby highlighting her intentions). Then, we would acknowledge that she is working to motivate employees to make the changes necessary to remain competitive and profitable (thereby highlighting her view of her impact). At this point, we would then indicate that her behavior strikes us as having a very different impact on her audience than what she intends. More often than not, this approach leads to a thought provoking message for the coachee, and coaches being perceived as credible and empathetic.

REFLECTION QUESTIONS

1. *Ivan hiring Arthur and Annie without Rick's approval and Rick's anxiety about Ivan being Bets's favorite are emotional triggers for Rick, causing him to temporarily forget about his efforts to change his own behavior. How is a victim mindset displayed here and how could you coach Rick to adopt a more accountable mindset? Can you think of instances where emotional triggers cause your coachees to forget about their coaching plans? What would it take for them to adopt a more accountable mindset in that moment?*

2. *Rick sarcastically introduced the feedback about Ivan's arrogant style by saying Arthur and Annie are, "just your type, Mr. Ivy League." What are the pros and cons of trying to generate realization through sarcasm? What other recommendations would you offer for initiating this conversation?*

3. Rick has repeatedly sent Stephan articles on micromanaging and delegating. What are the benefits and drawbacks of trying to create realization (awareness and accountability) through this method or approach? When would this approach work best?

4. Betsy reminds Ivan and Rick to work together as a team – the Karpos way. What impact does this have on the two of them? Why? How can this values-based approach be leveraged in coaching relationships?

5. People are very unlikely to change their personality through coaching. However, they have a decent chance of changing their behavior, even if it is related to their core disposition somehow. Think of someone you want to coach on a personality-driven behavior change and determine how to deliver this change message in a behaviorally-focused way.

6. Rick and Erin discuss the possibility that Ivan is tuning Rick out due to a lack of trust or credibility. We frequently find this to be a potential barrier to coaching. People don't take advice from people they don't trust! Consider an instance of someone you are trying to coach who tunes you out due to a potential lack of trust or credibility. What concrete actions or specific conversations can you engage in to enhance this trust and credibility prior to engaging in a coaching relationship?

CHAPTER THREE

GAS PEDALS AND PARKING BRAKES

The following Monday, Rick drops Joanna off at school and drives to work. As he opens the door and greets the receptionist, he notices two people sitting in the lobby.

"Annie? Arthur?"

Both of them get up immediately. Arthur is the first to shake his hand followed by Annie.

After exchanging pleasantries, they follow Rick into the office for introductions to the rest of the sales team. As the three of them turn into a wide corridor, they notice some hollering and high-fiving.

"Did we close with Fresco!?" Rick asks.

"Yes! Contract signed. It's final, after all those back-and-forths," Stephan pipes up. "Great work by everyone here!"

"That's huge! Way to go!" Rick reaches for a fist bump. "We'll make our April numbers after all! Oh hey," he recalls the new employees and turns around. "This is Arthur Caulfield and Annie Chung. They're our new analysts. They'll be sitting between Product Sales, Customer Experience and Marketing to better integrate our data activities. They're database whizzes so we will be heavily involving them in analytics. Arthur and Annie, why don't you start here and spend some time with our sales team, getting to know them and what they are working on. After that, they can take you to IT and get you set up with your computers and such."

Rick begins making his way to his office when he pauses, recalling what Erin said about showing Ivan that they are on the same team. He changes direction and knocks on the door of Ivan's office.

"Ivan? Arthur and Annie are here. They're spending some time with the Product Sales team at the moment, but they should talk to you and your team as well."

Ivan looks up, slightly surprised. "Oh, great. I'll be out there soon. Thanks for telling me."

A few hours go by as Rick sits through a somewhat dull company webinar on the innovative features of their latest SB-30 panels then starts digging into Ten Zero's account, one of their largest, to prepare for their meeting at the end of the month. He makes a phone call to Ten Zero's procurement department and checks in.

Outside his office, Stephan asks Arthur and Annie if either of them would be comfortable putting together on a report on poly panel sales trends and drivers. Arthur, dressed in a white-button down shirt, a blue blazer, with nicely combed over hair, immediately volunteers. He asks several questions that Stephan doesn't quite know how to answer, so Stephan asks him to hold on while he checks in with Rick.

"Hey Fisher, do you have a minute?"

Rick nods and Stephan walks in, saying, "I was talking to Arthur and he's going to take the lead on the poly sales report. I'll give him some context for my region, but he was wondering what exactly Bets wants from the report."

"It's the usual. She wants to know why this dip is happening and if this is consistent with what's happening in the industry at large. Basically, she wants to know if this is a trend we should worry about."

"Okay, that's what I figured."

"Then there's no need to ask me next time," Rick says supportively. "You know what to do."

"Yes, but I just wanted to double-check. If Bets gets unhappy with the report because she feels like it's not answering her questions…"

"Then she gets mad. But I will run interference if that happens."

"Ok. I know it trickles down, but as long as I have your support, I can handle it. Thanks Rick, I'm going to head back."

Stephan closes the door, walks over and debriefs Arthur. While he is talking, Arthur seems fidgety and Stephan keeps hearing some kind of muffled noise. "Anyone else hear that?"

"Oh, that's just my phone vibrating," Arthur says, removing it from his pocket.

"Do you have a call you need to take?"

"No, it's just various app notifications. Don't worry about it," he says as he swipes his screen a few times.

Stephan continues, explaining the difference between poly, mono and thin-film panels, while Arthur checks his phone some more.

"I'm sorry, Arthur, could you please put that away on silence?"

"It is on silent."

"But, *actually* silent. I don't want to hear it again." Stephan turns to Annie. "Annie, why don't you work with Arthur on the report? I'd like the report to me by Wednesday. I'll send you both a prior example of a report that you can reference as you pull the information together. There's more work coming down the pipeline, so stay tuned."

While Stephan is facing Annie, Arthur pulls out his phone and fiddles with it.

"Oh, there's Ivan," Stephan says. "I'm sure he has something for you two as well. He'll take you over to IT after you're finished."

Stephan heads back to his desk, relieved to have one less thing on his plate, but also anxious that Arthur will not be able to deliver. Arthur seemed a bit too distracted by his phone. Was he even listening? He is just about to sit down when Rick walks up to his cubicle.

"Hey, Stephan. May I ask you something?" Rick asks. Stephan nods, curious to see what Rick will say.

"What did you mean by it 'trickles down'? I said something about Bets being mad and you mentioned something trickling down..."

"Oh, it's nothing," Stephan shifts around uncomfortably in his seat. "I don't know what I was saying, really. Don't worry about it."

"No, I'm not upset," Rick clarifies, leaning his arm on the edge of Stephan's cubicle. "You know, I've been trying to be more reflective and thoughtful about my behavior lately, so I am genuinely curious what you meant."

Stephan looks at Rick closely and asks, "You're looking for feedback?"

"Yeah, I guess I am."

Rick notices that Stephan seems uncomfortable so he suggests they go for a short walk to the post office since Rick has a few packages to mail to clients.

"Fisher, you know that I'm thankful for giving me this chance at Regional," Stephan begins to say as they walk out the building.

"Oh, cut the crap, Stephan. My ego's big enough already," Rick says, joking to lighten the mood.

"That's true! This is just the first time I've ever heard you ask directly for feedback," Stephan says, smiling. "What I meant when I said that it trickles down is that sometimes when Bets is stressed she takes it out on you and you then tend to take it out on us. It's trickle-down-stress."

"Right, that makes sense," Rick replies. "How does that impact you as a manager?"

"It definitely affects how I manage. When you're stressed and you're on me, asking a ton of questions about how a certain deal is going or why certain trends are happening..."

"It's hard for you to feel like you can let go of responsibilities," Rick finishes the sentence.

"Yes, exactly," Stephan says, with a new bounce of energy. He starts opening up more. "Which is why I hear what you've been saying, and I am trying to delegate, but when I respond, 'I'll get back to you with an answer,' to a question you have, you don't look happy at all. That tells me that you expect me to know all the answers all the time, which I can't do if I'm doing what you've asked and delegating and not micromanaging."

They get to the post office and Rick opens the handle of the blue kiosk and drops off his three packages. He pauses and turns to Stephan, "Thank you for telling me that."

Stephan sighs in relief. "You know, we talk all the time, but I feel like this is the first time we're having a real conversation."

"Yes, it feels that way, doesn't it?" Rick says. "I admit that sometimes I do get stressed and since I trust you, I dump a lot of what I get stressed about on you. But I guess what I want you to know is that I go to you because I trust you."

"Thank you for saying that," Stephan says. He pauses, deliberating as to whether to say one more thing. "And if I can be real for one more minute..."

"Go ahead."

"It feels like there are two versions of you. There is the 'you' that goes out to lunch with me and tells me that I need to let go and delegate. Then there is the 'you' that emerges after you have a bad meeting with Bets or a bad call with a client and that 'you' wants very different things. So I'm not always sure who I'm reporting to sometimes, and I try to err on the safe side."

"There's Fisher," Rick smiles. "And then there's Rick."

Stephan laughs, "Yeah, Fisher eats fish tacos for lunch every day and brags about his daughter. Rick eats numbers for lunch and says, 'I want an answer in an hour.'"

"Okay," Rick says. "I'd like to think more about what you said. It has been quite a week, to be honest."

"Can I make a suggestion?" Stephan is feeling bolder. "I think we should actually ask Annie or Arthur to make the first proposal of what our Arizona campaign should be about. They should dig into the data and give us a recommendation. I know it's my region, but the truth is I know California much better than Arizona because I started there. At this point, if I look over the data, I don't know if I'd add much more value than one of them."

"That's not a bad idea," Rick holds open the door to the building for Stephan to walk in. "Let's do that. Because if I'm going to be honest myself, Stephan, I have been a little worried about whether you are ready for Regional. I know your team has good numbers, but I can't help but wonder if that's because you're helping them too much. That's partly on me though. I need to hold you accountable more for how you manage people and less about the status of certain details. For you to have success at this level, you need to lead more than execute. Your leadership needs to be more scalable. Does that make sense?"

"Yes. I know you took a chance on me and I intend on proving myself in this role. Thanks for understanding and for being clear," Stephan replies as they go up the elevator together. There is an awkward moment of silence before he says, "How is Joanna's team doing in the playoffs?"

Rick relaxes and goes off on his usual ramble on the Chasers and Joanna's batting statistics. After they get off the elevator, Stephan spots Annie in the corner. She appears to be helping Mary, one of the sales team members, learn certain functionalities of their CRM.

"Annie? You've got some bandwidth?"

Stephan explains to her why the Arizona campaign is happening and what they need from it. At the end he asks, "Did Ivan have any work for you?"

She responds. "Yes, he wants me to assess which of our competitors have gone out of business in Florida and put together a map so we can pitch geo-targeted services to residents there. I just finished it, so I was helping Mary. I hope that's okay."

Stephan smiles. "That's fine. We can use more people like you around here. If you can give me a draft of the Arizona campaign by end of this week, that'd be great. I'll check in with you in a few days to see how it's going."

❖ ❖ ❖ ❖ ❖

Three days later, at 6:30 AM on Thursday, Rick wakes up to an email from Bets addressed to him and Ivan. The subject line reads, "What's the latest on Ten Zero? Huddle at 9 AM sharp." The body of the email is empty. Rick sighs and lies back down for a moment to gather his thoughts for the day. He now has this meeting and several client calls before picking Jo up from practice today. He is excited to tell Erin about the breakthrough conversation with Stephan. He hasn't broached the topic with Ivan again, so there's not much to update there. Sometimes he wonders why he even bothers trying with folks like Ivan.

Mentally preparing himself for another day's dose of elitism from Ivan, Rick looks into the mirror as he shaves and repeats his mantra "I'm a team player…It's the Karpos way."

At the 9 o'clock meeting, Betsy is visibly tense. She says that Todd told her that Ten Zero may be flirting with cheaper panel options for their newest commercial developments at last night's fundraiser. Rick adds the news that he got very vague answers from Ten Zero's procurement when he asked about their thoughts on solar, but he made sure to update them about the latest SB-30 panels and emailed literature over.

"I listened to that webinar on our latest panels," Ivan says. "And to be honest, I think they're more style than substance. Sun Deck's panels are way more durable and weather-resistant than these SB-30s. And it's good that we're able to capture more data, but it's just not as sexy as this startup I read about, which uses predictive modeling and machine learning to automatically tilt solar panels throughout the day to maximize sun exposure."

One thing Betsy doesn't appreciate is a dig at the quality of Karpos's products.

"So then, Ivan," she begins as she slowly takes off her glasses to look him in the eyes. "What is *your* plan for Ten Zero?"

Ivan looks a little frozen. He and Rick were supposed to meet tomorrow so that he could get the down low on Ten Zero. He had pushed off any strategizing on this account until then and focused on other priorities.

Rick can tell that Ivan isn't prepared and he can't blame him. This meeting was scheduled last minute. He thinks quickly.

"Ivan and I discussed this. We're thinking of pitching them lifetime servicing, and if they pay top-tier, we'll throw in discounted upgrades for our latest panels," Rick says, darting a quick look at Ivan.

"Ah, that's a clever bundling," Bets replies, leaning in. "I want to hear more about this."

"Oh yes," Ivan recovers. "We'll get you more details early next week. It was actually mostly Rick's idea."

"All right, this meeting is less than a month away. Let's remember that $5 million dollars is on the line."

As they leave the meeting together, Ivan gives him a nod and quietly says, out of the corner of his mouth, "Thanks for that in there."

Rick shrugs. "Don't mention it. The meeting was last minute and I didn't want Bets to pounce on you just because of that. I know you would have something good to say if you had enough time to prep."

"I know. I really should have reached out to you to connect earlier though," Ivan says. "I dragged my feet when I shouldn't have. Thanks again for covering for me. Not many people here would have."

"I know we've butt heads a little bit," Rick takes the opportunity to say. "But I do want to say that, while I still feel you are pretty damn cocky, I've always respected your contributions and what you have to say. You have a different way of operating and I'm glad you're here to help us."

Ivan looks rather taken aback and nods slowly. "Thanks for recognizing that. And to tell you the truth, I've been trying to figure out why most people don't see that."

Rick says, "Well, remember the Executive Team meeting we had last week?"

Ivan laughs, "Oh yes I do! Everyone ganged up on me."

"Honestly, I thought your point about making some sort of public response to the new tariffs made a lot of sense," Rick says. "I think sometimes it's hard for people to recognize that because they're put off by your communication style. They think you're being condescending by comparing them to your old company and always trying to look like the smartest person in the room. If you make some small tweaks here and there to the way you deliver your messages, you may actually get through to them. It's not like you have to overhaul who you are as a whole person, so that's good!" he adds with a humorous tone, to try to lighten the conversation.

Ivan pauses and says, "You know, when you gave me that feedback last week about my communication style, I thought it was a lot of hot air, but then I started paying attention to people's facial and verbal reactions when I speak. I can see what you're saying."

Rick can't restrain his eyebrows from rising. "Was this really happening?"

"Although, it's hard for me to spend my brain cells thinking about small things like my tone when I've got much bigger things to worry about, like preventing this company from tanking," Ivan adds.

Rick reminds himself what Erin said about incentives. "It's definitely annoying, Ivan, and you're right, you've got a tall order on your shoulders. But think about what it would be like to propose an idea and have five people on your side instead of five people fighting you. It would make it so much easier for your plans to actually be executed."

Ivan barks out laughing and says, "That'll be the day! Oh hey, before I forget, do you have any favorite live music bars around here? I love live music and I've been trying to find a go-to spot in San Diego."

Rick tells him what he knows and heads back towards his office. For the first time in a while he doesn't feel annoyed or peeved after a conversation with Ivan. He mostly feels sad for Ivan, who seems to be digging himself into a hole here at Karpos, despite being one of the smartest people they've ever hired. Although Ivan didn't exactly come around, he did seem a lot more receptive than normal to what Rick had to say. "Baby steps," Rick tells himself, as he turns and heads into his office.

❖ ❖ ❖ ❖ ❖

At 7:30 PM, Rick is gathering his things when Betsy pops her head into his office. "Fisher, I've noticed that you and Ivan are getting along better," she says, with one eyebrow slightly raised. "I'm happy to see that. We really need you to come together for the Ten Zero meeting in a month's time. Can I ask what's changed?"

"Oh," Rick says, organizing his desk self-consciously, hoping this conversation doesn't take too long as he doesn't want to be late. "You know, there's always an adjustment period with each new person."

"So nothing happened? I want to know because there are some other folks here who could use an 'adjustment' with Ivan as well."

"Well," Rick says, "It's not all me. I have been talking to a friend and getting tips for improving workplace relationships."

Betsy leans back and crosses her arms, one hand holding her laptop. "Ah, so you have an office 'shrink' now to help you deal with your feelings, Fisher? Going soft, are you?"

"No, that is not what's going on at all. Just a buddy I met at Jo's softball games who's gone through similar stuff," Rick responds, defensively. "And I think investing in developing better workplace relationships is really important, actually."

"Of course," Betsy smiles to Rick's increasing embarrassment. "Hey, if it's making a difference in how you relate to Ivan, I'm all for it. Before I forget, what's the latest with the poly sales report? Or Arizona strategy?"

"We've asked A&A to take it on—Arthur and Annie—so let me check in with Stephan. We'll have something for you on Friday."

Betsy nods and leaves Rick's office, before turning around to say, "One last thing, I heard that Jo's team is in the playoffs?"

"Yes!" Rick smiles. "In fact, I'm headed to her practice soon. We finally have a shot at the Spring Championship for the first time since Jo's been at her high school!"

"Well, congratulations," Betsy smiles warmly. "After, what, five years of hearing your stories about all her softball exploits and her homeruns, I'm glad she's finally got a shot at winning something big. If I remember correctly, when you started here she was starting middle school, so she must be, what, a junior by now?" she asks.

Rick nods, "Yes, so it's a really important year for her. Lots of college scouts are paying attention during playoff season."

"Keep me posted. Especially if she needs any advice. My son, Kevin, played college basketball for a few years and I'm sure he'd be happy to chat," Betsy says, before striding out of Rick's office, laptop in hand.

Rick exhales and grabs his briefcase with one hand, holding his baseball cap with the other. "That is classic Bets behavior," he thinks to himself, smiling and shaking his head. Two weeks ago, she was chewing him out and today she's checking in on his daughter. As he walks towards the exit, he notices Stephan, looking fairly stressed and asks what's going on.

"Oh, Arthur is late with the poly report. I told him Wednesday and he said he needed more time to understand how our system works. Something about how our technology is too slow and outdated. Then he left at 4:45 to go to a yoga class, so I'm just taking it over. It'll be faster that way."

"Ugh, typical Millennial. Unfortunately, Bets wants something by tomorrow," Rick says, feeling his stress-levels rising as well. He recalls his conversation with Stephan over lunch earlier this week. "But don't stress. I'll tell her we need more time. It's not that urgent anyways. How about the Arizona campaign?"

Stephan lightens up. "Annie just sent me a draft proposal for the Arizona marketing campaign ten minutes ago. I've skimmed it and it looks very good, but still needs some minor tweaks. I'll work with her to polish it up and email it to you and Marketing tomorrow."

Rick is tempted to follow up with questions about Arthur, but he looks at his watch and realizes he has to go. "OK. See you tomorrow, Stephan."

❖ ❖ ❖ ❖ ❖

Later at practice, the Chasers struggle during their scrimmage against the Tigers. Afterwards, Rick manages to catch Erin and tell her about his conversation with Stephan.

"That's great to hear, Rick!" Erin exclaims. "I had a very similar situation with a direct report back in my pharma days in New York. The poor guy was always running late to things and I couldn't figure out why until I realized that I was always giving him last-minute things to do, which delayed him. Although he knew I was unhappy with his tardiness, he figured that he'd rather me be unhappy with him about that than be unhappy with him for not doing everything I told him to do immediately. When that clicked for me, I felt like slapping myself upside the head!"

"Yeah, it's exactly what you said – it's about Incentives—the incentive to change has to outweigh the incentive to keep doing what you've always done."

"And what about Ivan?"

"Actually, we also had a mini-breakthrough today. I saved him in a meeting with our boss and he was very grateful. He told me he's been more mindful as to how people perceive him, but he really doesn't seem to care all that much. He feels he has 'more important things to spend his 'brain cells on'," he says with an eye roll.

"Well, hang on. It's big news that you did that! How did you find it in yourself to shift your attitude towards him?"

"I didn't want to be soft with Ivan, and I'm definitely not going to start flattering his ego, but I want this company to grow and actually think we need what Ivan has to offer to get us there. I realized I had to start treating him as a member of the team."

"That's a very hard and mature thing to do. Congratulations."

"Don't congratulate me just yet! I'm not sure this will make a difference."

"Don't be too discouraged. There is another element to my coaching approach: Pressure. Have you ever made a new year's resolution that you never followed through on?"

"The real question is what New Year's resolutions have I ever followed through on!" Rick chuckles.

Erin laughs, "Yes, they are better called New Year's disappointments. But, that's it, you know, sometimes people know they need to change and they know why, they just don't make it priority. They don't feel any pressure to 'change soon or else.' I often think of pressure as a ticking clock that increases the urgency of whatever goal you are trying to reach. The atmosphere among our team during the 9th inning, for instance, is very different from that in the 1st inning when the game has just started. That's because we're all aware that time is running out.

"Look at Joanna. She really turned around. Not just because she understood why it was better for the team and for her, but also because there was a very concrete window of opportunity. If her team made it to the championship, scouts would be there and she would get a chance to 'wow' them. Only when she recognized this did she really start to pay attention to what I was saying about batting strategy."

Rick ponders this for a while and nods, "It's like what happened to me and my diet. I've known for a long time that I have to eat less meat, but it wasn't until my doctor said that I would be at risk of dying early from a heart-attack that I started making drastic changes." He adds quietly, "I want to be here for as long as possible and I feel the clock ticking, especially since Melissa passed."

"Joanna talks about Melissa a lot, and I can tell that despite her complaints about you, you're a good dad," Erin says, looking him in the eye. "And I'm glad you brought up that point about your diet. Ripeness varies by task, not by individual. You were ripe for change when it came to your diet then, but it took you awhile to be ripe when it came to shifting your approach to Ivan. People can be ripe for one task but not another."

Rick considers this. "You know, that's true even for Ivan. When we interviewed him, he expressed some reservations about moving here because he's always seen himself as a 'Bay area' kind of guy. But since coming to San Diego, he's really plunged right into the local scene, asking for recommendations so he can find the things he likes here."

"Ah, so he was ripe, for whatever reason, for change when it came to adapting to a new city. The tricky part is being open to change when it comes to his collaboration style," Erin responds.

The two chat for a little while longer before wrapping up their conversation so Rick and Joanna can load up their car and head home.

TAKEAWAYS AND TIPS:

This chapter is full of vulnerable moments between Rick and Stephan, Rick and Ivan, and even Rick and Erin. The truth is that while change is often imposed from on high – the boss, the doctor, the company – making a change really is a personal decision. People have to personally invest in a change to really implement it. Thus, simply giving advice to "delegate" or "change your communication style" is not typically as helpful as digging deep to understand someone's motivations and incentives.

The second letter of the RIPEN model is "I", which stands for Incentives. Incentives are a fairly complex matter. There is the incentive to change—which can be to gain certain positive outcomes ("if I do this, it'll help me get promoted") or to avoid certain negative outcomes ("If I don't do this, I could get chewed out"). It can be prompted by external carrots or sticks (money, or decreasing influence with specific people or departments) or by internal values and beliefs (loyalty or a desire to produce for a company or individual). If incentives are the gas pedal in a car, think about how you can utilize your coachee's incentives to "hit the gas pedal" and motivate and drive them to action.

There are also counter-incentives that prevent people from changing or encourage them to maintain their status quo. These are akin to the parking brakes on a car, preventing it from moving. When people aren't changing their ways, chances are high that it's for a reason. The status quo is clearly working for them in some way. Maybe people don't want to change because they fear punishment for not knowing the answers or not being as on top of things as they used to be, as in Stephan's case. Whatever the situation is, it's always worth examining not just what incentives a person has to change, but what counter-incentives she or he has to *not* change. Fear of change, risk of failure, and complacency are common examples of counter-incentives.

Although we are introducing one element of the model at a time, in reality, the process of change is rarely linear. People move back and forth between each element, depending on the context. "Incentives" are the focus of this chapter, but they certainly come into play throughout the whole process. Additionally, you may have noticed that Ivan is still slowly going through his realization, observing how people are reacting to him and realizing how he comes across. He may not care at this point (or assume accountability for changing the behavior yet), but we will see if that changes in the future.

For now, we've learned that the feedback messenger sometimes matters as much as the content of the feedback itself. Ivan probably would have taken feedback more seriously if it came from Betsy, but since Rick was a peer, he had to use other means and build trust with Ivan to show him that he is trying to help, not sabotage him.

IN THE MEANTIME, IF YOUR COACHEE LACKS THE INCENTIVE TO MAKE A CERTAIN CHANGE, HERE IS A SERIES OF RECOMMENDATIONS FOR YOU TO CONSIDER.

- Ask yourself what truly motivates this person. What are the values and beliefs that are most representative of them? Can your coaching somehow enhance the extent to which they believe they are maximizing their values? One way to tap into these values is to ask your coachee to identify 3 different situations in their life when they have felt the greatest sense of purpose or personal engagement and identify the patterns that exist across these examples.

- Encourage the coachee to look at the broader impact he or she is trying to have at work or in life. Have them explore how their status quo behaviors are *inhibiting* them from realizing this impact. Next, explore how the new behaviors identified could *maximize* the likelihood of realizing this impact. To further understand counter-incentives, they should reflect on the perceived risks associated with changing their status quo behaviors. Ultimately, it is up to them to decide if truly realizing their desired impact is worth abandoning the comfort of their status quo behaviors.

- What external motivators are important to them (money, job security, promotion, visibility, the opportunity to do a certain type of work or work with like-minded people)? How can you link Incentives to these internal and external motivators?

   For example, a young, high potential, exceptionally ambitious and results-oriented leader received feedback that his hard charging style was turning off his peers, particularly those in other departments (who had different goals) or in different countries (who had different cultural norms). They responded passive aggressively toward him, hindering his ability to get results, thus hindering his upward mobility. Once he realized the link between changing his approach and his career trajectory, the new behaviors were very quickly adopted and maintained.

- Have you maximized enough of the "universal" motivators, such as the desire to be respected and appreciated or to maintain autonomy and control over one's environment? While everyone has unique motivators based on their specific personality, culture, and goals, we also know that certain motivations are universal factors that apply to everyone in some way.

- Have you asked the person directly, "What would motivate you to make this change?" While most people, us included, are not expected to have perfect insight into their own motivations on every behavior ever engaged in, many times coaches fail to ask what motivations for change one has in a single, particular instance. This is a simple and great place to start!

- What is the likelihood that the change your coachee makes will actually result in the outcomes *they* want versus those *you* want? What is the likelihood that not making this change will have drawbacks that matter to your coachee? Are there ways of enhancing the likelihood of realizing these positive or negative incentives?

- As a coach, it can be helpful to create a list of common incentives that you have seen in others. Use this as a cheat sheet to remind yourself of the broad range of possible motivators, or as a multiple-choice list, describing common motivations, to explore with the coachee. This helps put ideas and feelings into words since many people have a limited vocabulary of descriptors when it comes to incentives and motivation.

- It is critically important to explore your coachees' counter-motivations. What concerns them about making the change? Unspoken psychological barriers are one of the most under-leveraged aspects of unleashing maximum motivation ("I would love to delegate more, but doing so means I would have time to focus on strategy, which is not a strength of mine, and I don't want to be exposed as less valuable and credible").

  One way to identify counter-motivations is to ask your coachee not only to think about incentives to change, but also about compelling reasons not to change and/or the perceived risks they associate with making this change.

- Focus on the emotional components of Incentive, not just the logical and factual aspects. If a promotion is the motivation to improve in an area, focus your next set of questions on "why" they want the promotion, not just on the promotion itself. Is it money? Respect? Security for their family? Understanding the "why" and the emotions behind the obvious surface level incentives will result in identifying a more powerful lever to pull on.

REFLECTION QUESTIONS

1. *What steps or actions did Rick engage in to build trust with Ivan? How did this impact Ivan's openness to Rick's message? Why? How might this apply to your coaching clients?*

2. *Rick tells Ivan that he is "pretty damn cocky," but then says that he has always respected his contributions and what he has to say. This balanced message enables Ivan to hear the feedback in a manner more consistent with his view of himself. Why is this important? What is the impact of this "both/and" approach?*

3. *Rick highlights to Ivan that he simply needs make small tweaks to the way he delivers messages in an attempt to make his feedback behavioral rather than about personality. Why is this approach more likely to be successful?*

4. *What incentive does Rick explore with Ivan to encourage changes to his communication style? What incentives can you identify for your coachees that matter a great deal to them versus to you?*

5. *When Rick broaches the subject of Stephan's delegation challenges, he asks a question using Stephan's own words, "What did you mean when you said 'it trickles down"? He then uses a follow-up question rather than defending himself to Stephan's reply ("how does that impact you as a manager?"). This opens Stephan up to a more robust discussion than did the articles Rick sent in the past. Why is this development tactic more powerful?*

6. *Initially, Rick and Stephan share a good level of trust. In this chapter, their trust goes a level deeper. Why? What are the implications for your coaching?*

7. *In what ways do you see Rick taking accountability for Stephan's delegation challenges? How does this impact Stephan? How might you apply this to your coaching work?*

8. *What important incentives seem to drive Stephan? How does Rick tap into these in his discussion with Stephan? How might you uncover the incentives of your coachees, which often go unspoken?*

9. *Do you notice any counter-incentives causing Rick, Ivan, and Stephan to continue their counter-productive behaviors? How are these addressed in the story? What counter-incentives cause your coachees to maintain their less-than-ideal behavior despite being aware and incented to make a change?*

CHAPTER FOUR

THE CLOCK STARTS TICKING

A ringing melody plays near Rick's bedside. He reaches over to his night-stand, grabs his phone and turns off his 6:30 alarm. Normally, he would hit snooze, but today he is looking forward to getting up.

For the past month or so he'd been living out of a suitcase, traveling all over California, Arizona, Texas, and Florida, looping back through San Diego for a few crucial meetings and to catch the start of Joanna's playoffs. He hasn't had much time to focus on any of the changes he had been working on. Beyond weekly phone calls with Stephan and meetings with Ivan, his focus has been exclusively on their top-tier clients and partners.

Although he hasn't been paying close attention, he has been feeling that things are getting better between him and Ivan. He has tried to include Ivan more in client meetings, and Ivan has done a decent job promoting Services without undercutting or dismissing Sales. Ivan has also been involving him more in strategy meetings and emails with his team…and with Betsy.

That said, aside from Rick and Betsy, Ivan has not changed much towards anyone else. During a joint-conference call last week with Sales & Services,

Rick saw the Sales chat channel buzzing with messages like, "Remind me why we hired him again," and "Email me when Ivan stops talking."

Clearly, no one in Sales is a huge fan of Ivan. When Rick saw those messages last week, he quickly responded, reminding people of the larger mission and, why it is important for Sales to share information and clients with Services. He wasn't sure this had any real impact though. Even Stephan, who usually tries to keep a positive attitude about people, dropped a complaint about Ivan during their check-ins.

Stephan, however, has been trying to step back and let his team take the lead more. The Southwest region's numbers are coming along well without any red flags.

Overall, Rick is looking forward to returning to the office. There's plenty of work to do. The Ten Zero meeting, scheduled for June 28th, is now two weeks away. It could be a huge win for Karpos. Depending on how it goes, it could prove to Betsy and the board that he and Ivan can work together effectively, and that the new strategy is viable. Ivan and he have yet to set aside enough time to align on a game plan for that meeting though, partly due to scheduling reasons. Ivan has been traveling a lot this past month as well. But now, they are both back in town.

He opens his iPad and starts reading through the news, starting with Sports then Politics. An hour later, his daughter emerges.

"Good morning, Jo. Remind me, is it the semi-finals or quarter-finals tomorrow night?"

"Quarter-finals, Dad. Can't you read? The schedule is on the fridge."

"This means the Spring Championship will be coming up in two weeks then?"

"June 29th," she affirms.

Rick checks his calendar on his phone. "Alright, obviously I'll be there. I'm not traveling for awhile anyway. Get dressed soon. I want to beat the traffic to school."

❖ ❖ ❖ ❖ ❖

At 9 AM, Rick walks through the door of Karpos's offices and, much to his surprise, only a few people are there. He walks over to the sales corner to greet his team, but only sees a handful of people, including Stephan. He strolls over to Stephan's desk to catch up.

"By the way, how are Annie and Arthur doing?" Rick asks him halfway through the conversation. "I heard them present their reports on that conference call a few weeks ago, but wasn't able to hear Annie well. I couldn't tell if it was a technical issue or if it was her."

"Oh, yes," Stephan sighs. "It was probably her. Her report on Arizona solar trends was great! I read it. But when she presented, she was super quiet, faltering and umming all over the place. It was a little painful to watch. People were tuning out by the end."

"A pity," Rick replies. "Arthur presented well, though. He sounded confident and articulate."

"That he was," Stephan says. "Until it came time for follow-up questions. Someone asked him how we should respond to Tesla's solar roof tiles and he froze. Surprisingly, Annie chimed in with a great response."

Rick responds, "You know, my daughter is like that sometimes. She writes great papers, but chokes in front of a crowd. I think these younger generations — since all they do is text or tweet, and never pick up the phone and call – have lost some communication skills."

"Maybe, although I feel bad for Annie. I could tell she was pretty disappointed after her presentation. I think she just needs a little bit of coaching to improve," Stephan says and checks his watch. "Oh hey, we have that town hall coming up. I've got to respond to some emails before that starts. Let's talk later."

At 10 AM, Betsy convenes a company-wide town hall to talk about the "state of the company." Immediately, she jumps into sales being down and the short timeline they have to turn things around. A few people turn their heads to look at Rick. "Ah," he thinks. "It's always the sales guy who gets beat up once things turn sour."

She launches into a stern sermon on the importance of being customer-centric and how she isn't seeing enough "customer-centricity" reflected in their sales numbers and marketing, or in their IT processes and software.

Betsy then gives the floor to Ivan, who launches into a very well-polished presentation about rising home ownership of panels, which creates a bigger market for panel servicing. Lucinda, VP of Marketing, then speaks about their two latest marketing campaigns, one that touts the weather-resistant features of the newest Karpos panels and the other highlighting the risks of owning solar panels without properly maintaining them.

"Excuse me," Tony, VP of Engineering, raises his voice, with arms folded across his large chest, "It seems like these campaigns are at odds with one another. On one hand, we're saying our panels are the most durable and can take anything Mother Nature can throw at them. On the other hand, we're sounding the gloom-and-doom bells by talking about panels as if they will fall apart at any second if they aren't serviced."

Lucinda, with her eyebrows crossed, swivels her chair to address him. "Obviously, Tony, we'll be pitching these ads to different audiences."

Tony sighs and replies in an exasperated tone, "But how can we guarantee that people who see one ad will not see the other? Plus, our large clients, like Ten Zero, are building several new complexes and looking for a solar partner. We need to make sure we all have the same message." Tony jabs his finger into the table to emphasize his point.

Ivan quickly chimes in, "Rick and I are working very closely in preparation for that meeting. My goal is not to diminish the perceived quality of the panels in the slightest, but to position servicing as an added bonus that will make panel ownership even more convenient and cost-effective."

"Good," Tony grunts. "I don't think people appreciate the engineering behind these panels and how hard we've worked to make them high quality. And, as I'm sure you know, Ivan, we have a long history with Ten Zero. They were one of our first clients to take a chance on us a few decades ago."

"Right, of course," Ivan says, worriedly twirling a pen on his notepad. He knew Ten Zero was an old client, but didn't know it was one of Karpos's first. He then wonders who brought that account in, amongst the many other questions rising to the forefront of his mind.

Betsy says, "It may be good to have you call in for that meeting, Tony, if you can join. They'll appreciate hearing directly from you about the innovative features of our SB-30s. And Luce, have you chatted with Ten Zero about their feelings on appearing in some of the ads for our Arizona marketing campaign?"

Rick leans back in his chair and takes a glance of the room as the conversation continues. Although senior management is heatedly engaged in conversation, most of room seems disengaged. Some are on their phones while others slouch in their chairs, looking down on the floor. There are also more empty seats than normal at a company town hall.

"What's going on here?" Rick wonders. When he came in this morning, most people weren't at their desks. It also seems like half the office is dialing in for this town hall today rather than showing up in person.

After the meeting ends and people slowly trickle back to their desks, Stephan asks Rick if he is free to chat for a bit about prepping for the Ten Zero meeting.

"Hang on. I think Ivan should be part of this conversation." Rick says, calling Ivan over.

"What's up, team?" Ivan says awkwardly, as he walks up to join the huddle.

Stephan shoots Ivan an odd look. "I don't think this concerns Ivan directly," he says to Rick.

"Even so, it'll be good for Ivan to be in the loop," Rick replies, shrugging.

"Okay, sure," says Stephan. "Just wanted to get some advice. You know I have a very close relationship with the people at Ten Zero, but ever since I took over Regional, I've been trying to introduce them to my team. I'm trying to let go, as we've talked about, and delegate more, however, I just feel like they're dropping the ball. I know I can't manage that account relationship as closely as I did before, but Ten Zero requires white-glove handling because, well, you know their long history of customized requests and needs."

"Oh yeah, like what happened in 2014 with Erica and the botched order?"

"Don't mention it, man," Stephan groans. "Thinking about it is still painful. The thing is that I know them very well, but I'm trying to let go, as we've talked about. But I just feel like they're dropping the ball."

Rick can't afford for the Ten Zero meeting not to go well. "Dropping the ball in what way?"

"Nothing super big. It's little stuff, like missing opportunities to cross-pitch with Services, taking too long to get back to people and schedule a phone call, or just lacking the patience to deal with their specificity in their needs. I can hear it when I'm on these calls with them. I end up swooping in and smoothing things over."

Worried, Rick says, "But you're still on this, right? Do you think this will affect how Ten Zero shows up at the meeting in two weeks?"

"I don't think so," Stephan says. "We just have to make a decision about who's in the room for that meeting. It could just be you and me and Ivan, or maybe we include other Southwest sales folks."

Rick is relieved. "As long as we handle that meeting well, I don't care who's in the room. We can make the call a few days before. It's no big deal."

"Got it," Stephan nods. "We have a call coming up next with a few Ten Zero folks to walk them through our latest panels. It's not a senior meeting."

"Can I listen in as an observer?" Rick asks.

"Yep, I'll forward you the invite," Stephan replies, turns and walks back to his cubicle.

Ivan looks at Rick and says, "Hey, you doing anything for lunch?"

"I was going to pick up a few slices from this vegetarian pizza joint I know."

"Mind if I tag along?"

"Be my guest. Most people here wrinkle their noses the minute I say 'vegetarian' so I never have company," Rick chuckles, gesturing towards the front door.

They walk out and head over to a pizza joint. Ivan and Rick decide to split a large artichoke and eggplant pizza. After the waiter takes their order, Rick lifts his water glass to take a gulp, sets it down and clears his throat.

"Before I forget, I just want to say you did well in the town hall this morning. I think people appreciated the fact that you respect the quality of our products. Tony's very proud of the SB-30s we just released."

"Don't mention it," Ivan says, looking a bit embarrassed. "It doesn't make sense to undercut our product in front of the client."

"Glad we're on the same page."

"Listen," Ivan says, adjusting his V-neck sweater. "Over the past month, I've been thinking even more about what you said about my 'communication style,' as you put it. It hasn't been my top priority, admittedly, but now that we have this big meeting coming up with a long-standing client, I know I've got to lean on your team and others a lot more since you all know Ten Zero's history much better than I do. I know solar very well, but have no clue what happened with Erica in 2014, for instance."

"It might better if you don't know," Rick laughs, extending his legs from under the table. "Save you from the scarring."

"I'm sure," Ivan smiles, raising his head to catch the eye of a passing server. "Excuse me? Could I get sparkling instead of tap water?" adding a bit too loudly, "I can't believe they didn't offer the option initially," once the server leaves.

"Right," Rick says, unsure what to say. "Anyways, you just need to sit down with Stephan, his Southwest team, and Tony to get the intel on Ten Zero. They can bring you up to speed."

"I guess. I don't know though…" Ivan trails off.

"Why are you feeling hesitant?" Rick puts on a quizzical look. He remembers what Erin told him: Don't push answers. Let him come to his own conclusions.

"I'm not sure how much people like Stephan or Tony want to help me beyond the basics. I get the sense that they want to keep me at arm's length."

"Ah," says Rick.

"Look, you know I don't have a habit of asking for help. I'm not here looking for pity. I'll be fine. But I could use your advice on how to improve the perception people in the office have of me and get them on my side for once."

Rick's hand, holding a slice of pizza, pauses in mid-air. Erin's words float back to him: When the student is ready, the teacher will appear. "Is this what she was talking about?" he wonders.

"I'm so glad you asked, Ivan," Rick says before taking a bite and wiping his mouth with a napkin. He refrains from launching into a satisfying monologue and instead asks, "What questions do you have?"

"Well, for starters, I notice that when I speak up in meetings, people either roll their eyes or tune out. What can I do to prevent that?"

"The good news is you don't have to overhaul your personality or change the substance of what you say, which is usually very solid. It's more about making small tweaks, like not always referencing how things were done at your old company, or giving people credit too often for the contributions they've already made. It comes off as condescending."

"Okay, here's what I don't understand," Ivan sets down his glass of sparkling water. "I chose to come here. Obviously, I believe in Karpos. If I didn't, I'd still be at Sun Deck. Why don't people get that? I really think people are too insecure and easily offended here. I'm certainly not trying to be condescending to anyone."

"No, of course not," Rick says, eyeing the clock. He is supposed to be at a sales and marketing meeting in five minutes, but this conversation with Ivan is too important. Besides, Stephan will be there, so he can handle it.

"Ivan, I'm not here to debate you over your intentions or whether you're actually condescending or not. All I'm saying is that this is how people here perceive you. And, if you want them to listen to and work with you, then you've got to accept the fact that this is how they feel about you and start from there. Because, even if you are right and people here are insecure, what does that matter? What's the point of being right if no one is following you?"

Rick realizes now that his voice has gotten a little too loud. He is a little surprised by himself. He did not expect all of that to come out. Feeling a little nervous now, he waits for Ivan to react. Ivan seems lost in thought. His hands are pressed together, leaning his face against them.

"Okay, keep going. I want another example of how I come off as condescending," Ivan finally says.

"Um, well," Rick says, breathing in deeply. "Remember this is not about changing you, it's about changing how people *perceive* you. You… tend to be very vocal about how slow our IT systems are every time you use them."

"But your systems are so slow!"

"Notice that you used the word 'your.' Why not 'our'? This is your problem too now."

"Fine, I'll adjust my language. And I do see it as my problem too! That's why I make a big fuss about it! What else am I supposed to do?"

"For starters, maybe loudly complaining to everyone within earshot and walking over to the IT corner and grabbing the first person you find isn't the best way to go about things. You've got to follow our ticketing process for reporting bugs. It's slower that way, but that's how things are done here. We follow protocol."

"And, if you don't mind me asking, why should I care about protocol?"

"Because that's how you show respect for Karpos, Ivan," Rick replies firmly. "The processes that we follow here have worked for decades and have played an important role in our success to date. Don't get me wrong, our ticketing system could be improved. I agree, but bring that up with our head of IT directly and privately, not in front of everyone in a meeting."

Ivan takes a deep breath in and crosses his arms. "This is not how I'm used to doing things, but I'm listening."

"It's going to be hard, but you're doing it already. Recall what you said to Tony at the town hall. You assured him that you were going to respect the quality of our product."

"So more of that stuff?"

"Yes, along those lines."

❖ ❖ ❖ ❖ ❖

Rick and Ivan keep talking for another forty-five minutes over lunch, discussing interpersonal dynamics, but also strategy for the Ten Zero meeting, and eventually head back to the office. As Rick enters, he spots Annie walking out.

"Late lunch?"

"Yes," she says, looking a bit embarrassed. "I got caught up with finishing a report. The town hall took a bit longer than expected."

Her mention of the town hall prompts Rick to ask, "What did you think of it? It was your first one here at Karpos, right?"

She nods, "Yes, it was very informative. It was helpful to hear from Betsy directly since I don't interact with her very much."

"And... what did you think of people's reactions? Especially to what

Bets was saying."

"Um…"

Rick looks around and lowers his voice. "You can be honest with me. I was noticing a few things, but I just want to make sure it wasn't just me."

Annie turns the question around. "So what did you notice?"

"Oh," he replies, "I thought half the room was disengaged, on their phones or just slouched in their chairs. And there were so many empty seats!"

She adds, hesitantly, "I noticed that too. I wasn't sure if that was normal or not, given that it was my first one."

"What do you think's going on? Do people just not care about this company? Why don't people—" Rick is about to keep going before he stops himself and course-corrects. Take responsibility, he reminds himself. "I'm not saying anything bad about anyone. I'm sure people have their reasons, but I just want to better understand what's going on and if there is anything I can do to help turn it around."

"Well," Annie thinks for a while before continuing. "It seems that people are feeling overwhelmed. In all confidentiality, I've had a few people give me the head's up that things have changed at Karpos, and now they are now expected to do their same job plus much more, like learn new skills and understand a new market without much guidance, support or resources. It's discouraging and some people are checking out, I think."

"Oh, I see. That's very helpful," he replies. "And your confidence will be honored. I won't mention who told me this, but I hope it's okay if I relay this feedback to Betsy. It may be important for her know this."

Annie looks a bit worried and says, "I just don't want this to get back to me. But yes, do tell her. I think she should know."

"Fisher!"

Rick turns around to see Stephan standing behind him. "Fisher, I thought you would be at the meeting!"

"Lunch with Ivan ran long," Rick says, shrugging then turning around to wave bye at Annie.

"Oh? You got into another big argument?" Stephan raises his eyebrows.

"No, actually, he was asking for advice, believe it or not," Rick says. "I think he's buying into the Karpos way more now."

"I'll believe it when I see it."

"Hey, I wanted to say," Rick changes the topic. "I managed to catch the end of the marketing meeting yesterday. I thought Arthur was very impressive there. He sounded good. Annie could use some work in her delivery, although, as usual, she had great things to say. I find her very insightful."

"Yes," Stephan says, putting his hands into his slacks. "I think Annie could get better, but once again, it was painful to watch her. As for Arthur, I just wish he turned his report in on time. I could've gotten that report done in half the time he took."

"And they say Millennials are all about efficiency," Rick smirks. "But don't start thinking that way. You're not supposed to do these reports anymore. We've got help for that now. It's just about managing A&A."

"Right, right. I've got to head into another meeting. Catch you later." Stephan says, turning away to his desk. Rick walks back to his office, ruminating over his conversation with Ivan. He still feels that Ivan is a horse's ass, but he also feels cautiously hopeful. If Ivan could make some small but meaningful changes, perhaps others would start buying into his ideas on how to improve Karpos.

❖ ❖ ❖ ❖ ❖

Shortly after 5pm, Rick gathers his things and starts to head out of his office. Almost everyone else is gone by now, except for Betsy, Ivan and Stephan, which is a bit unusual. He knocks on Betsy's door and hands her the reports on poly sales and Arizona's marketing campaign that Annie and

Arthur put together.

"Thanks, Fisher," Betsy says without looking up.

"Don't stay up too late, Bets. Almost everyone's gone now."

Betsy looks up at him and takes off her glasses. "Yes, indeed. I've been noticing that people have been leaving before 5 PM in the past few months. It's ridiculous! How can we turn this company around if everyone is clocking in late and clocking out early?"

"I'm only leaving because it's Tuesday and my daughter has a game tonight…"

"Oh shush, Fisher," Betsy says. "I know that. You've also been staying late multiple nights and been on the road for the better part of the past month. I'm talking about the others. Where is your sales team, for instance? I hope they're making calls even at home."

Rick adjusts his stance uncomfortably. Should he even bother getting into it with Betsy? He could tell her what he observed earlier today at the town hall and how he's been noticing an overall decrease in morale. But he knew that Betsy would demand an explanation for his observation, and he wasn't sure he knew the answer.

"We need new blood, that's what we need, Fisher," Betsy says, putting her glasses back on. "People are getting too lazy and apathetic around here. They're not hungry."

Rick can tell that Betsy is done with the conversation, so he quickly says, "Sure, let's talk about this more next time. Sorry that I've got to go."

"One more thing."

Rick turns around warily.

Betsy peers down at Rick from her glass, "Joanna's a junior, right? So what she is thinking about for college? I imagine she's being recruited with all her legendary home-runs, or at least, so I hear from her father."

Rick relaxes his shoulders. This is the side of Betsy that he's missed, the side that cemented his loyalty to Karpos.

"Oh she is and there is definitely interest, but I think most of the scouts will show up for the Spring Championship."

"And how's she doing?" Betsy leans over to ask.

"You know," Rick replies, "She's hitting well. Not as many homeruns as before, but more RBIs actually. They got a new coach who's really helped with her batting strategy."

"Ah," Betsy leans back to say. "That's a big shift, requiring a whole different kind of technique and mental calculus."

"Oh, yes," Rick says. "Actually, the hard part hasn't been the technique as much as her willingness to change it. She's always been a power-hitter."

"Oh, I know. I know. It's interesting that she's been able to change up her style."

"Yes, it is a big change for her," Rick replies then turns to grab his bag, hauling it over his shoulder. "Bets, I've got to run if I want to catch the start of the game. It's the quarterfinals and the Chasers are up first, so I don't want to miss her at-bat. Gotta be there to record her for her highlight tapes, you know."

"Go get 'em," Betsy says, immediately casting her attention back towards the papers in front of her.

❖ ❖ ❖ ❖ ❖

Two hours later, after a homerun and an RBI-single by Joanna and a great diving catch by their centerfielder in the 9th, the Chasers pull off a win, 6-5. Rick is elated, in part because he managed to remember to pull out his phone and record her hits. "These videos will be great footage for college scouts," he thinks.

After the game, he manages to catch Erin while she's walking to her car.

"Jo did great, didn't she? And, great job to you too, Coach!" Rick exclaims with a wide beaming smile.

"Thanks, she was great! Very strategic hitting. How are you doing?

How's your own coaching going?"

Rick hesitates. "We don't have to talk about my work, you know. I feel bad taking up your time with all this stuff."

"Don't worry about it. The only way I got better at coaching was because people took time out of their regular day-jobs to help me. I have plenty of great mentors in my life. I'm just paying it forward."

"Well, thank you. I am sincerely grateful," Rick says, unsure what else to say. "I'll make this fast. You won't believe the conversation I had with Ivan."

He quickly details the discussion that Ivan and he had over pizza earlier today.

"So," Rick concludes, "I don't know what did it but I think it was that Ten Zero meeting coming up. I think he realized that he has to depend on others for it, so he needed to change how he related to people or else he would be heading up a river without a paddle. Until this lunch, talking to him has been like talking to a wall."

"That's amazing, Rick," Erin says. "Like I said before, when the student is ready –"

"The teacher will appear," Rick finishes. "I know, I thought of that during lunch." He thinks for a moment and adds, "I think another turning point was also when I told him I wasn't there to debate whether or not he's condescending. Rather, just to tell him that if he wants to work with people, he has to work with the reality of how they perceive him, even if he disagrees. That really shifted the conversation from him trying to defend his intentions or attack the legitimacy of other people's reactions, to him trying to figure out how to practically adapt to our company."

Erin lights up. "Really smart move there! It absolutely helps to make the feedback less like a personal character attack. So do you still think that Ivan is a bad egg who'll never change?"

Rick laughs, "Did I ever say that? I don't think I said that exactly."

"Well, you certainly meant to say it, even if you didn't," Erin smiles. "And what about Stephan? How is his managing going?"

"I think it's been all right," Rick says, unconfidently, looking down at his shoes. "To be honest, I haven't been paying that much attention to him. I've been caught up with strategizing for this meeting with Ten Zero coming up at the end of June and handling some other key reports."

"This is that big client meeting you've been talking about?"

"Yep, it's huge."

"Will Stephan be there?"

"Yes, of course. Actually, that reminds me, he did mention something earlier today about how he was disappointed in some of his sales colleagues for dropping the ball with Ten Zero. He secured that client, but now he's a bit too busy to handle that relationship so he's trying to bring others in to do so."

"What was he disappointed by?"

"I don't remember specifics, something about how he's disappointed with their performance and how he's had to 'swoop in' at the last minute."

"Is that what you want him to do? Swoop in at the last minute?"

"Honestly, I just want this meeting to go well. And if he has to intervene, so be it."

"Sure, okay," Erin says, folding her arms and staring at him.

There is a pause, and Rick finally exhales and says, "Okay, I know what you're thinking. Stephan can't keep doing this. And there's no way he can do as a good a job as he did handling that relationship now that he oversees the whole Southwest team."

"You said it, not me," Erin says, smiling and unfolding her arms. "I wonder why Stephan is still struggling to manage at this level."

"Yeah, come to think of it, he still makes comments like, 'It'll just be faster if I do it,' far too often for my liking. I've been trying hard on my end to not get on his case though. For example, one of our analysts turned a report in late that was supposed to be due to our CEO, and Stephan was worried about it, but I told him I'd tell her that we need more time."

"It sounds like you are doing what you can to support him," Erin replies.

"What gives then? He clearly realizes now that he needs to change, he has the incentive and the pressure. He knows that he's essentially being watched to see if he can handle this position. What's missing?"

Erin pauses and turns her gaze towards the softball field. "When Joanna started shifting her batting strategy, she had to get out of some bad habits. Even though she was mentally committed to changing, her body was so habituated to make these big, deep swings that it was tough getting her to adjust her swinging technique depending on what she wanted to do.

"I remember once," Erin continues, "she got very frustrated during batting practice. It was an exercise where I would tell her where to aim her hits—left field, right field, line drive, second base, etc. She tried, but wasn't very successful, so she basically gave up halfway through."

"What did you do?"

"I gave her a pep talk and she turned it around immediately."

"No way."

"Of course not," Erin snorts in laughter. "It was weeks, if not months of hard work. Watching videos, replaying videos, breaking down her swing, practicing. It was very humbling for her to seek out help. But eventually, she got better and became more confident in her abilities."

"I see," Rick leans back on his feet and looks up into the sky. "She couldn't just flip a switch and change overnight."

"Stephan, I take it, is one of your top-performers, that's why you promoted him?"

"Oh yes."

"And what makes him so good?"

"So many things," Rick says, turning around to look at her. "He is always on top of things. I always feel assured whenever I give him a task or responsibility that it will get done, no matter what, and on time too. He goes above and beyond to help others. You can never ask a question that would stump him. He's always prepared."

"But now he's managing a large team…how many exactly?"

"30 or so."

"Yeah, there's just no way he can be on top of everything or have all the answers to all the questions. He has to re-wire how his brain has been used to functioning for the past however long he's been at Karpos. He needs to redefine what excellent performance looks like and build the skills and habits to support it. And that, my friend, takes time and coaching."

"I honestly think Stephan is doing well. He's super competent. He gets what he has to do. I doubt he's struggling that much."

"If you say so," Erin shrugs. "But if you notice that something's off and you want to give him some advice, be concrete. Talk through specific scenarios and how he could have handled them. Here's where you really want to break it down a bit more and draw a map so he knows how to get from Point A to Point B. But don't browbeat him. The key is to boost his confidence and raise his expectation that he can do this, that he can lead others."

"Is this the next part of the model?"

"Yes, actually. It's the letter 'E' for Expectation. Expectation is about self-efficacy—the ability to accomplish a task *and* one's confidence in the ability to do the task successfully."

"You've been holding out on me!" Rick says, laughing. "So far it's R-I-P-E. When can I learn the full model? Isn't there one more letter?"

Erin smiles and shakes her head. "I save that one for when I feel that people really need to hear it. Every time I say it, people immediately gravitate towards that one and forget the rest. Anyway, it's almost nine so we should get going. I'll see you at the next practice."

Rick nods, "Catch you later. Thanks again, Erin."

✔ TAKEAWAYS AND TIPS:

The literature on behavior change – in business, psychology, medicine – shows that knowing you need to change (Realization), and why you need to do so (Incentive) may not be sufficient to tip someone into action. Pressure is often needed and is the "P" in the RIPEN model.

As Erin says, think of pressure as a ticking clock, counting down the time remaining to make a certain change. As a manager or leader, ask yourself if there is sufficient pressure, such as, "Can making this change wait until next week? Next month?" If the answer is yes then your team may not feel any urgency to make the changes you want. Without pressure, some people tend to shelve behavior change and keep it on the back burner.

Pressure is associated with an urgency driver that causes someone to make specific changes in the near term. It can take many forms. In Ivan's case, it was a fast approaching opportunity with a big client. It's also worth noting that the fear of appearing ignorant in front of the client triggered Ivan much more than other incentives, such as being nicer so others want to work with him. This is an example of Ivan's key value system dictating which form of incentive will have impact. Prior to this chapter, recall that he waved away Rick's feedback, saying that it was not "high priority" for him as he had other things to spend his "brain cells" on. For some of our clients, a large organizational change caused them to start scrambling. For others, a new boss overseeing them or an opportunity to interact with C-suite executives motivated them to kick things into gear.

As we hinted at towards the end of this chapter, applying pressure without giving people tools and resources to change (raising their Expectation) can backfire. People need to feel that they can indeed pull off the changes that need to occur. If not, they may simply feel guilty and discouraged. Betsy's leadership style is a classic example here. She is great at cracking the whip and lighting a fire under people (Pressure), as she did in the town hall. However, it does not seem to be working very well, evident in the fact that Rick is reluctant to approach this topic with her and not everyone is aligned with her marching orders. We will get a chance to see if that changes in the upcoming chapters.

HERE ARE SOME STRATEGIES TO ELEVATE THE PRESSURE LEVEL FOR OTHERS IF THEY APPEAR TO BE HESITATING TO TAKE ACTION, OR SEEM TOO COMFORTABLE WITH THE STATUS QUO ON A SPECIFIC BEHAVIOR CHANGE.

- Ask what conditions would be necessary to feel like this issue was urgent? What needs to be true to feel pressure to make a meaningful change *immediately?*

- Ask them to change their perspective by adopting the point of view of someone who *does* think this change is urgent. What would they say? Have them reflect on why they see it as less urgent than the other person does.

- Create a "false" deadline. If they think this change is something that can wait until next month to start making, change the deadline for them to create urgency, which at first will be obviously false, but can stimulate them into real action (and this momentum can overcome the lack of inertia they previously had).

- Create escalating penalties associated with delaying the behavior change. Alternatively, create mini-rewards for achieving small wins towards the larger change. This approach mixes Incentive with Pressure, and this combination of dynamics often creates action.

- Build commitment by having them announce their intention to make a change. Public peer pressure is a powerful motivator, especially for coachees with a healthy ego and desire to maintain social status.
- Put the coachee in a position where they will have a natural deadline with big consequences.

  For example, a CIO has a very siloed team member, who admitted the need to get better at "working across the matrix," but never did anything about it. The CIO assigned this person with leading a key presentation to the executive team the next quarter, knowing that they could only be successful with the help of two other colleagues in other departments. It turned out that the pressure of the impending boardroom spotlight was exactly what was needed to feel enough Pressure to actually go talk to other colleagues.

REFLECTION QUESTIONS

1. *Ivan is feeling enhanced pressure to act on Rick's feedback given the impending, important meeting with Ten Zero. In our coaching work, we often see such pressure points cause people to pivot from intellectualizing about one's development to actually taking action. Consider your specific coachee's development goals. Is there any way to enhance the pressure or urgency that will cause your coachee to pivot from reflection to action?*

2. *Like many coachees, Ivan gets hung up on what his intentions are versus how he impacts people ("I'm not trying to be condescending…people at Karpos are so sensitive. If I didn't believe in the products and the company why would I be here?"). A powerful way of communicating feedback and coaching is acknowledging the coachee's intentions while highlighting how their behavior is actually having a different impact than what they intend. Why might this approach be effective in terms of creating more openness to trying new behaviors?*

3. *What has transpired in Rick's efforts to coach Ivan that have opened Ivan up more to Rick's guidance than earlier in the book? What behaviors has Rick demonstrated? Why has Ivan's view of Rick shifted?*

4. *In Stephan's case, the impending meeting with Ten Zero drives pressure. Too much pressure – without the supports to succeed – can cause him to want to revert to his typical ways of behaving (providing hands on guidance) because of his anxiety associated with failing. As a coach it is important to observe how people react to these pressures and highlight that these are the critical points in time that determine if someone is actually able to make sustainable behavior change.*

   Pressure is a good thing, but too much pressure without a way to actually succeed can cause paralyzing anxiety. How might you utilize such pressure points to support your coaching work? How can you avoid paralyzing your coachees with overwhelming levels of pressure?

CHAPTER FIVE

THE HELP HOTLINE

Rick! How's it going?"

Rick pauses and turns around in Karpos's parking lot to see Arthur trailing behind.

"Oh, hi, Arthur. I didn't see you there. What's up?"

"Not much. I had a good weekend, how about you?"

"Good. A lot of softball practice. My daughter's team made it to the semi-finals. They won last Tuesday and are playing tomorrow night."

"Oh, I used to play baseball. That's so cool that your daughter does that. I miss those days. I was a pretty good pitcher back then!"

"Nice," Rick says, opening the door and holding it for Arthur. "By the way, good job on that presentation a few weeks ago. I dialed in and I thought you presented well."

"Thank you, Rick. That means a lot coming from you," Arthur replies, pausing before he continues. "So, I hear there's a big meeting coming up with Ten Zero on the 25th."

Rick nods, curious why Arthur mentions this.

"May I ask who will be at that meeting?"

"Ivan, myself, Stephan, and Tony will dial in. Why?"

"Well, I was thinking that you should really have an analyst involved," Arthur responds confidently. "Someone who really knows the industry and regional trends and can wow them with knowledge of the data. I've been looking over the energy data we've collected through their panels and think I can make some smart recommendations."

Rick is a little stunned at Arthur's presumptuousness. "Um, we don't typically do that, but I'll check in with others to see what they think. I've been a bit out of the loop for the past month."

"Of course, I'm not saying that I should be the one at the meeting," Arthur says carefully. "But I'm happy to send along some of the reports I've done so you can see my work."

"I'm sure you do good work, but it's more that this is a pretty senior meeting so we just have to think about what's appropriate."

"Okay I'll forward along what I've done anyways so you can just take a look and let me know when you've decided."

"Sure…" Rick says, still amazed, a little annoyed even, at Arthur's audacity. "I'll take a look."

❖ ❖ ❖ ❖ ❖

They part ways as Rick heads into his office, sits down and dials into a video call with Ten Zero. Stephan and a few Southwest regional sales people are running it, and Rick, mindful of Erin's advice to pay attention to Stephan's management style, asked to dial in as a silent observer. Nytasha, one of the Sales managers on the call, has already started walking people through a PowerPoint presentation on the latest SB-30 panel data.

Everything seems to be going well until Ten Zero's people raise some tough questions.

"Stephan, can I ask why Karpos has not adjusted its prices when the cost of solar is going down in general? How can we ensure data security, especially in light of recent hacks? What's the latest on investing in extra security as we've discussed in the past?"

Rick observes as Stephan fields each question as they come. His answers are good, but he can't help but notice that Ten Zero acts as if Stephan is the only person on the call. Nytasha does try to deliver the first response to their questions, but each time, Stephan chimes in at the end with his comments on the topic."

After the call ends, Rick emails Stephan, "Listened in to the call. Swing by my office to chat?"

He ponders while he waits for Stephan to come, a bit surprised at the call. He thought Stephan was heading down the right track since their last conversation a month ago. He'd even told Erin last week that while, yes, there were some things he was concerned about, overall he had faith in Stephan to figure things out.

"So," Rick says, as Stephan walks into his office. "How did you feel that went?"

"I think they like the panels, but we may have to work on pricing and answering some data questions later on," Stephan says as he takes a seat.

"Let's get to that later. I want to hear how you thought Nytasha did."

"You know," Stephan sighs, "I feel like she wasn't as prepared as she could've been. Her presentation itself was fine, but her answers to their questions could have been better. I felt I always had to chime in to make a point she missed."

"Nytasha is one of the people you're trying to introduce and pass the Ten Zero relationship off to, right?" Rick asks.

Stephan nods.

"So my main concern, if you'd like to know, wasn't Nytasha's answers. Sure, they could have been better, but they were fine. I was more concerned that everyone on the Ten Zero team directed their questions to you, not

Nytasha, even though she was the one giving the presentation. How did you introduce her to the team in the beginning of the call? I missed the first five minutes."

Stephan looks a bit sheepish. "I... I just said that I was here with the rest of my sales team and that we were going to walk them through our latest panels. Then I asked Nytasha to take it over."

"So, you never introduced Nytasha explicitly or, better yet, let her introduce herself?"

"She's not a stranger to them; we've been in the same room before."

"Yes, but think about the message that sends to them: Stephan's in charge, everyone else is just taking orders from him."

"Look," Stephan, getting a bit flustered, says. "I didn't want to say this, but it provides helpful background. I stayed up until 11 last night correcting Nytasha's PowerPoint. It wasn't ready for prime time. The deck was fine, but it had to be excellent because it's Ten Zero, and because everyone in this company knows about this meeting and is watching. So, yes, I was a little nervous heading into the call, maybe overly so, but I had some reason to be.

"Nytasha's great, don't get me wrong. I've been frustrated with the whole team, not just her recently. I'm trying to delegate and let go and leave people alone, but I somehow always end up having to re-do work at the last minute. It ends up taking more time than if I just did it myself, which is—"

"Stephan, sorry to interrupt, but what kind of directions or guidance did you give her?"

"I gave her all the information. I told her who was attending, that this was a prep call for the big meeting at the end of the month, and that I needed her to present on our new panels."

"Did you ask her if she's done this presentation before? Give her ideas you had on how she could go about highlighting the panels' strengths and anticipating follow-up questions?"

"I thought she could handle it. You're always telling me to step back."

"Yes, but stepping back doesn't mean abandoning your team," Rick sighs. "It's not great to just leave them in the dark."

"But I asked her if she understood what I was looking for and she said yes. So, I left her to it. I assumed she was answering in good faith."

Rick can see that Stephan is getting frustrated and will likely not be open to whatever advice he has. He asks himself how he can coach Stephan to come to his own conclusions and gets an idea.

"Tell me," he asks. "When you had to fix Nytasha's PowerPoint last night, how did it feel?"

Stephan replies, "I wasn't happy, that's for sure. My wife was giving me a hard time earlier that day about not spending enough time with the kids, and there I was, working at 11."

Rick catches himself from saying, "Well, that's a choice you made to do that." Instead, he says, "Okay, how else did you feel?"

"Frustrated. Is this turning into a feelings session?" Stephan smiles in puzzlement.

"Bear with me here. Were you surprised that her deck didn't meet your expectations?"

Stephan pauses. "Not really, actually. I had a hunch she wasn't going to really deliver for the few weeks or so that she was working on it, but I didn't want to micromanage her and tell her how to do it. Remember that lunch we had a month ago?"

"Yes, I remember," Rick nods. "So if you weren't surprised, what did you feel instead? What would be the opposite of that feeling?"

Stephan looks at Rick quizzically. "I'm not sure how to put it. It's a not surprised feeling, like I knew this would be the outcome."

"It sounds like you felt somewhat validated that your suspicions were right?"

Stephan nods slowly.

"And although it is certainly frustrating to have to work late to fix things, it does feel a bit good to be validated, to feel like you really do know what's best after all, doesn't it?"

"Well," Stephan mumbles quietly. "I don't know if I'd go so far to say that, but sure…"

There is a moment of silence as Stephan takes in this information. Rick shifts perspective and says, "Look, you were clearly trying to do the right thing. And I know you're feeling a lot of pressure about this meeting—I'm feeling it too—especially since your promotion, which, I know, makes you feel like you're in the spotlight now."

"If I can be straightforward, it does feel sometimes like people are watching me to see if I truly deserved it," Stephan says.

Rick is a little surprised that Stephan seems to be feeling greater pressure than he expected. He changes the direction of the conversation. "I remember when I got my first big managerial promotion. I was 30 and working at a pharma company at the time. Before that promotion, I managed projects, but this was the first time I was in charge of people and their performance. And I remember feeling like I was scrambling all the time to cover different people's bases and fix their work.

"And what took me a long time to understand was that when I gave directions, people seemed to be signaling that they understood what I was looking for, that everything was good-to-go, but when it came down to the wire, it was clear that there was some miscommunication."

Stephan interjects, "That's exactly what happened with Nytasha and me. I asked her, 'Do you understand what I'm asking for?' and she nodded. So I assumed she was good and didn't want to micromanage."

"Now," Rick says, pulling his chair closer to the desk. "Imagine if Bets gave you a project and asked you that question. Let's say that you only clearly understood about 80 percent of it and were unsure about the other 20 percent. What would you say to her? Realistically."

"I'd probably say....no, I *would* say that I understood and then I'd ask my follow-up questions to others who may know the answers because I don't want to waste her time. She's the CEO and has bigger things to do than explain things to me."

"Maybe that's how Nytasha sees you a little bit. She's relatively new to Karpos and maybe she sees you as someone whose time she doesn't want to waste. And," Rick adds, "Let's face it. Even if people don't fully get it, no one wants to look stupid. So, they ask around, make assumptions or try to do some research on their own. You know, I even do that with Bets sometimes, to be honest. Many people on the executive team do it with her. It's not a great habit, but we still do it."

"I see, so you think that when Nytasha said she understood, perhaps she didn't *fully* understand?"

"Maybe. All I'm saying is that asking, 'Do you understand?' is like asking, 'Are you smart or not?' And most people are going to say yes, regardless."

Stephan rests his chin in his hand. "So what's a better question to ask then?"

Rick smiles. "Glad you asked. Ask her what she thinks the expectations are and what the deck should convey and look like. Ask her if she has everything necessary to deliver what you want then, schedule some time to check in with her to review progress and avoid scrambling at the last minute. That's better than leaving her to figure out a task alone, and having to swoop in at the last minute because she's not meeting your expectations."

Rick recalls what Erin said to him about re-wiring habits. He says to Stephan, "I know it's going to take awhile to adjust your habits. Take it one situation at a time. You're very competent, Stephan, you'll figure it out. But, let me apply my own advice here. Consider the call earlier. What do you feel like my expectations are about how you should have handled that? I want to make sure I'm being clear myself."

Stephan smiles, "This feels like I'm back in middle school or something. Ok, I'll do this meta-exercise. Let's see," he continues. "Introduce Nytasha properly so that people know that she's the one driving the call and answering questions, at least when it comes to the SB-30 panels."

"And if they ask follow-up questions?"

"Well, let Nytasha answer first and I'll chime in at the end—which I believe I did."

"Yes, but you added to her answers without waiting to see if Ten Zero's team was satisfied with them. How can you know if her answers were unsatisfactory or incomplete until you see how they respond, and how she handles their responses?"

"So when do I intervene then?"

"When you see that she doesn't know how to respond."

"How do I know that?" Stephan asks, and then lights up. "I know, maybe I can set expectations with her before the call so she can give a signal for when she needs back-up."

"That's a good idea," Rick replies. "Just be sure that you make clear that you're there for back-up only. Kind of like a "help hotline" she can call when she really needs you and wants your input." He continued by drawing an interesting comparison, "Just like you are wanting my help on thinking through this topic, I took that as a sign you were wanting my support, but if you had not seemed ready to hear it maybe I wouldn't have provided specific suggestions."

Stephan saw the point, "Gotcha. That makes sense. Be ready to pick up the phone, so to speak, but only when she "calls" for help."

Rick starts gathering his papers around his desk and stacking them into a few piles. "I trust you. Let me know if you need anything from me or want to chat more about this. I'm here to help."

Stephan leans forward in his chair. "There is one thing."

"Yes?"

"I have several more customers like Ten Zero I need to off-load to someone. My fear is that if Nytasha or someone else bungles those relationships and word gets out, Bets is going to look for skulls to crack and it's going to be my head. I know I'm basically being watched to see if I deserve my promotion. The stakes just feel high, that's all, especially given Karpos's current situation."

"That's on me, not you," Rick says firmly. "If the first few meetings with a client and your team don't go well, I've got your back. I'll make sure blame doesn't fall on you or someone on your team. That way there is room to make mistakes."

Stephan nods, gets up and says quietly, "I'd appreciate that."

As Rick watches Stephan leave the room, he leans back in his chair and reaches for his cup of coffee. It turns out that Stephan's empowerment of his team still has some ways to go. Things were clearly not going as well as he thought they were. But, he can't really blame Stephan. Ultimately, he is guilty of doing the same thing that he's calling Stephan out for: Issuing orders without sufficient assistance or guidance. Stephan is going to need more hands-on coaching as a senior manager than he originally thought.

Rick mulls over Stephan's feeling of being watched by people to see if he deserved his promotion. "Why did Stephan feel like that? Was this a signal coming from him or from others? Did he stress Stephan out too much by saying that he was worried if Stephan was ready for Regional? He thought it would increase the urgency and pressure around this area of change that Stephan needed to make, but perhaps he overplayed it."

❖ ❖ ❖ ❖ ❖

Later in the afternoon, Rick joins Ivan in a meeting with the head of IT to discuss vendor-selection for a new customer-analytics dashboard. During the meeting, Ivan, to the surprise of everyone in the room, not only refrains from any snide remarks, but actually compliments IT on their knowledge of the latest cyber security trends. Of course, Ivan still has plenty of feedback and constructive criticism to give, but his tone, Rick notes, is much improved.

After the meeting, Ivan says to Rick, jokingly, "So, how did I do?"

Rick is about to answer but holds back. "What do you think; based on people's responses to what you had to say?"

"Honestly, I think I did a great job, if I do say so myself! I felt like people were nodding and adding on to what I had to say instead of arguing against me or giving me looks."

Rick laughs, "Yes, it wasn't the 'Ivan versus everyone' show."

"I did notice though," Ivan says, "that the discussion seemed to die down after I voiced my opinion on which vendor I thought was best. I'm not actually certain on who we should partner with. I just wanted to add my two cents and hear what others had to say. That seems to be a trend here," Ivan adds. "I put forth a strong opinion and people take it to be the end of the discussion when that's not what I want at all. I love debate."

"Well, you usually do have something smart to say, and I'm glad to hear that you want pushback. Do you want to hear how I think you can better communicate that?"

"Yes, you're my Karpos-Sherpa," Ivan says, smiling.

"Try adding, 'that's just my opinion, what do you all think?' at the end of your sentence. See how people respond then."

"That's it?" Ivan snorts. "Those are the magic words? Okay, Fisher. We'll see if you're right. I'll see you later." Ivan turns and heads toward his office.

"Hey, real quick, before you go," Rick says. "Arthur basically asked me earlier this morning if he could join the Ten Zero meeting next Thursday. I thought it was a ridiculous idea, but I've been out of the loop for the past month. How did he get this idea? Did you talk about this with him?"

Ivan replies, laughing, "I certainly did not. That guy's got some chutzpah."

"Or entitlement. I would never have even thought to ask that when I was at his level. He's been here for what, little over a month? Does he think he can just step over all the people who've worked here for so much longer?"

"You know," Ivan says, cocking his head. "I haven't interacted with Arthur a lot, but I think he's got great communication and presentation skills so he may be client-ready. I actually don't think it's that bad of an idea to have a data person at that meeting. We may be able to impress Ten Zero with some insights and really show them the value we bring to the table. I'd ask Stephan what he thinks. He's worked with them more than I have. Oh, there he is!"

Ivan spots Stephan walking down the hallway. "Stephan? You got a minute?"

Stephan walks over and Rick catches him up on what he and Ivan have been discussing.

Stephan rolls his eyes, "Once Arthur starts turning his reports in on time, I'll be happy to entertain this idea."

"But what do you think of what Ivan said?"

Stephan pauses and crosses his arms. "It might be a good idea. But I wonder if it should be Annie instead of Arthur."

"Annie? Didn't she botch a presentation a few weeks ago?"

"Yes, but hear me out," Stephan says, pausing to collect his thoughts. "Arthur is good in front of a room, but Annie works twice as hard, knows twice as much and doesn't get the same credit. She always handles the follow-up questions and knows solar inside and out."

"But…"

"And," Stephan says, looking at Ivan, "You know from our debrief last Wednesday, Ivan, that Ten Zero has a history of being extremely particular about what they want. We only put up with it because they order so much from us. They're definitely going to come at us with a million questions like they did on the prep call Nytasha and I had with them."

"Actually," Ivan says, "did I tell you what we ended up doing with Annie's report on Arizona solar trends? It was so good that I had her rewrite it as a thought leadership piece, which we polished up and sent to our big Arizona partners and customers, including Ten Zero."

"Really? And?"

"They loved it. They want to see more of that from us. I actually think we can really impress Ten Zero with how well we know them and their region if we have Annie at the table."

"Yes," Stephan adds, "she's got to work on her presentation skills. We have, what, eight days before then? I'll work with her to improve. I'll have her present in front of you two and Bets, and if she can pull that off, I bet Ten Zero will be doable."

"Okay," Rick says. "But why do you care? I mean, sure having her there might help, but why do we need to rush things so that she can be there?"

"Just let me try this," Stephan says. "You guys can make the call when she presents in front of you."

Rick replies, "Okay, if there's one thing I've learned over the past few months it's that people can surprise you. Just don't dump this opportunity on her. Be sure to coach and work with her to accurately set her expectations about herself."

Stephan says, smiling, "I got this, don't worry, Fisher. Also, you're sounding more and more like Yoda these days. What's in your water?"

Ivan laughs, "Fisher's become my personal Yoda too."

Stephan lightly pokes Ivan with his elbow. "So *that's* why you've been acting different, huh?"

"Just ask Fisher," Ivan says. "He's like my Yoda-on-dial. I text him whenever I feel someone is being an idiot and am not sure how to handle it."

"Stop it, guys," Rick says, embarrassed, and changes the subject.

❖ ❖ ❖ ❖ ❖

The next day, Stephan calls Annie over to his desk and tells her about the opportunity to attend the Ten Zero meeting next Thursday.

"Oh, me?" Annie says. "Are you sure?"

"Yes, you," Stephan smiles. "Although, I want you to present in front of Bets, Ivan and me next Monday. If you meet their standards, they'll be much more open to having you at the client meeting. What do you remember about my feedback from your last presentation?"

"You told me to make more eye contact with everyone there, straighten up, speak up in general, and slow down."

"Do you have some time now? I was thinking I could walk you through some more concrete tips."

"Sure. I think that meeting room in the corner is open. We can huddle there," Annie points out.

Stephan walks Annie through his feedback on her body language, volume and tone of voice, and verbal presentation tics.

"Okay, so let's say you're presenting your report in front of me, Ivan, Bets and Fisher. I'll keep time for five minutes. Go ahead."

Annie starts with an overall description of trends in Arizona weather, solar production and energy consumption, current state tax incentives, and upcoming regulatory battles they anticipate. Her presentation is much improved compared to her previous try, but there are still some kinks to work out, particularly around vocal intonation.

When she's finished, Stephan remarks, "Much better. What's going through your head when you're standing there, presenting?"

"Um, not much, just what I'm going to say next."

"Yes, but what's the next layer of thought underneath that? Don't think about it too much, just answer."

"I guess I'm looking around and thinking about who's in the room and what they are thinking of me as I'm speaking."

"So rewind to the meeting we had where you presented your report.

What did you think when you were looking around at those people in the room?"

Annie thinks for a while with her eyes cast down towards the ground. Stephan notices her silence and adds, "Would you believe me if I told you that I used to be super nervous every time I had to turn in a report or memo to Rick or Betsy?"

"No way," Annie smiles for the first time in their conversation.

"Oh yes! Writing stressed me out like nothing else. I'd stay up late proof-reading and editing, even my emails, over and over again. I didn't want anyone to be able to hold up something with my name on it and point out a mistake. Of course I'm better now, but writing is still something I always try to avoid."

"Wow, for me it's almost the exact opposite," Annie replies as she starts to loosen up. "Writing is where I can be this detached voice and no one has to know who I am or what I look like. But," she adds, "I totally feel the way you did when it comes to public speaking. I feel completely vulnerable. I can see people's reactions to my mistakes in real-time. There's no hiding. I've been terrible at public speaking since I was young."

Stephan laughs. "I actually love public speaking. We should swap notes. Maybe you can teach me a thing or two about writing."

"But your writing is great! Why were you worried about it?" Annie asks.

Stephan replies, "My writing is not excellent, but it's as good as the next guy's. I've just always felt the burden to be twice *as good*, not just as good, as the next guy."

"Why is that?"

"Because, frankly," Stephan says, looking at Annie in the eyes, "I know that people are going to be looking for mistakes. They don't expect someone who looks like me to do well. Whenever I'm in a room I'm always conscious about who's there and who's not."

Annie pauses then asks, "Can I be honest? When I was standing there, giving my presentation, I was thinking about the same thing; how much I stood out in comparison to everyone."

"In what way?"

"In how… no one in the room looked like me. I'm sorry! I'm not saying this to complain or make a big deal; I was just answering your question."

Stephan smiles, "I'm not here to get you in trouble, Annie. I'm trying to help. Please go on. How did it feel when you thought to yourself that no one looked like you?"

"Well," Annie thinks about her words carefully, "When that thought hit me, my brain just froze. All I could think about was how everyone was staring at me, and how I was going to disappoint them."

Stephan looks kindly at Annie. "Do you know why I advocated for you in front of Rick?"

She shakes her head.

Stephan says quietly, "When you don't see yourself reflected in the room, you start to doubt whether you belong in the room. You work extra hard to prove that you are competent, that you do deserve to be there.

"And that's how, as a black man, I got to where I am now. Ironically, now I have to work on shaking some of my old habits. Although, I'm somewhat high-up now, the feeling that I've got to prove myself never goes away entirely. I have the sense that this may be how you feel too."

"Yes, yes," Annie nods, wide-eyed. "No matter how well I do, I somehow always feel like I'm tricking people into believing that I'm good at my job. I just imagine people closing the door on me, saying, 'Wow, she's actually bad. Can't believe she's even working here.'"

"I can assure you that in all the closed-door meetings I've been in where you've come up, everyone has been happy and grateful that you're working here. I know it's hard to feel like you belong, especially when there aren't many Asian American women in Karpos, but I'm going to personally do what I can to help.

"So," he says, rolling up his sleeves, looking at the clock. "It's almost five now. If you have to go, it's not a problem. But if you want, I'm happy to coach you on public speaking."

Annie nods and takes out her cell phone, "That would be great. Let me just text someone to tell them I'll be a little late to dinner."

After she does so, Stephan says, "Okay, I want you to present one more time in front of me—not the whole thing, just the first five minutes. Before you start this time, know that everyone in the room thinks very highly of you. Imagine how that feels and let it sink in. Take a deep breath then start speaking." They continue talking for well over an hour, discussing writing, speaking, communicating, their families, and backgrounds before wrapping up for the evening.

❖ ❖ ❖ ❖ ❖

At 6 PM, Rick leaves his office and makes the 30-minute drive to the softball fields. He's running a little late, but makes it in time for the start of the second-inning. To everyone's surprise, the Chasers win by a lot, ending with a score of 8-3. Joanna doubled and singled twice, bringing in four of those eight runs.

After the game, Erin finds Rick in the stands and waves.

"Rick! How are ya?" she says loudly. "Did you already have that big meeting with that client…Ten Eleven?"

"Not yet, the Ten Zero meeting is next Thursday," Rick says, walking down from the stands to meet her.

"Listen, Erin, I just want to say thanks for your advice last week," he says when reaches the bottom of the stands. "What you said about changing habits and how it takes time was another lightbulb moment for me. I had a great follow-up conversation with Stephan where we really got nitty-gritty. And, Ivan's even been texting and asking me for advice throughout this past week or so! Look!" Rick proudly holds up his phone, showing his text messages with Ivan.

Erin smiles and gently pushes the phone away, "You're an adult. I don't need to see that; I'll take your word for it."

Rick laughs and puts his phone away, "I'm just still so surprised that I look at these text messages every once in awhile to remind myself that this is happening. So, are you feeling ready for the championship next Friday?" he asks. "Congratulations on coming this far!"

"Yes," Erin replies, turning her gaze towards the girls packing up their bags and leaving the field. "Who would've thought we'd come this far, especially since we barely scraped our way to the playoffs."

"But," she adds, opening a water bottle, taking a chug and wiping her mouth, "I do feel like we're ready. We've gone through some big changes as a team and we trust each other. How about you? How is your team feeling about the upcoming meeting?"

"I feel like we're all finally coming together as a team too. The one person I'm not so sure about is the CEO. She asked, just yesterday, to join the Ten Zero meeting. We have a good relationship, but she's been on edge lately. If things start to go off-track during the meeting, I'm worried she'll blow."

"You haven't talked about her in a while," Erin says.

"I know. I've got my hands full between Ivan and Stephan and some Millennials that I have to manage now too."

"How does she lead people? If I recall, there's a lot of change going on at Karpos. How has she been leading folks through it all?" Erin asks, as she unties her ponytail, combs through her hair then loops it back into a ponytail.

"You know," Rick says, looking up into the dark sky. "She's really good at providing the reasons for change. She's made sure we all know the business case for pivoting our business model."

"So she's good at getting people to realize what needs to change and clarifying why it's beneficial to both them and the company. That's Realization and Incentive, or at least her version of what their incentive should be," Erin adds.

"Yes, yes, and she's even better at Pressure. She knows how to crack the whip and convey a sense of urgency. Nothing moves slowly around her. Everything's urgent all the time."

"Okay," Erin studies Rick's facial expression. "Your face seems clouded. What's up?"

"I think," Rick says, drawing words carefully out of himself, "That's she's not so great at the last bit: Expectation. She doesn't do much to bolster people's expectation that they can pull off the change that she wants. She kind of leaves people feeling demoralized or stressed about whether they can meet her expectations, giving little to no guidance."

"Ah. So she asks for a lot from everyone, but doesn't offer much support."

"Exactly… oh no, no, Erin," Rick groans. "I see where you're going. Don't make me bring this up to her. Remember I tried more than a month ago, but she dismissed me completely. She told me I was going 'soft' for caring about feelings and relationships."

"I didn't say anything," Erin smiles.

"But I can see that you're getting ideas. I'm telling you I don't think she'll ever change. She's always been this way."

Erin shrugs her shoulders, raises her hands and says, "Your boss is often the most difficult relationship to manage. But of course, if you never bring it up then she may never change, and you will be in the same position down the road, trying to meet her high expectations without guidance."

"True, I can't argue with that," Rick says, as he starts to turn away and look for Joanna.

"Hear me out, Rick," Erin says, drawing Rick's attention back to her. "If you do want to broach the topic, do something similar to what you did with Ivan, but even more sensitively. Don't make it about whose perceptions are objectively right, but about working with peoples' subjective perceptions since, ultimately as a leader, she has to lead them."

"Sometimes I think she'd rather just fire a bunch of people and get new blood in than work with existing employees."

"Remember the 80/20 rule I talked to you about early on in our conversations?" Erin asks. "It sounds like she thinks 80% of the people at Karpos are hopeless and only 20% are salvageable."

"Yes, that sounds familiar. I used to think that too. Now it's more like 75-25," Rick smiles and winks at Erin.

Erin laughs. "So we've made 5% improvement, I see."

"I'm kidding…partly," Rick replies. "We'll see how this meeting goes. It'll be the real test of many things—Ivan and me, Stephan and his team, and Bets and us.

"By the way," he adds, "You never said what to do with people who you think actually aren't likely to ever change on a certain issue; the 20%. You said once, 'When the student is ready, the teacher will appear.' What happens if the student is never ready?"

"Oh, yes," Erin says, nodding. She pauses, studies Rick and says, "I think you're ready for the very last letter in the model: 'N.' I've been holding off on sharing this because most people fixate too much on this letter. It actually stands for two words, 'Natural Inclination.' Some people have a higher natural inclination for change than others. A lot depends on how one defines themselves, especially, their successes and failures."

"What do you mean by that last bit?"

"Do you see your success as a result of your natural talent or of hard work? Similarly, with your failures; Do you see them as reflective of your natural limitations or as opportunities to grow?"

"I would have to think about that one for awhile. I can think of a few people who probably have low natural inclination."

"Just bear in mind that people with low natural inclination – those who aren't open to change and see their successes and failures as fixed things – can still change, but they've got to be really *ripe* on all the other factors. Think of it like the direction of the wind. Having low natural inclination is like having a strong headwind blowing against you, making it harder but not impossible to make forward progress."

"Ah, yes, like Ivan, I think."

"Yeah, he's a good example. The opposite is true too. Having high natural inclination means that you have a tailwind, propelling you forward and accelerating your momentum.

"Remember that when we first started talking about Ivan, you had written him off as a lost cause, someone who would never change. You even had doubts about Stephan! I try not to share the last letter of the model until I feel someone is ready because the default interpretation people tend to have is that someone is not coachable because they have low natural inclination, instead of taking it as feedback about their coaching skills. And, as you can see, tweaking your coaching style can actually make a big difference even for people with low natural inclination."

Rick spends a few more minutes chatting with Erin before meeting Jo at the car. They talk about batting techniques on the way home, but part of Rick is still mulling over his conversation with Erin.

✓ TAKEAWAYS AND TIPS:

If Realization, Incentive and Pressure are factors affecting motivation for change, Expectation is a factor that influences the belief that change can occur. It's the E in the R-I-P-E-N model.

"Expectation" is our layman's label for the academic concept "self-efficacy" or a person's belief in their ability to achieve a certain goal. Psychologist Albert Bandura, the pioneer of this concept, explains that people with high self-efficacy or a high level of Expectation are more likely to view difficult tasks as something to be mastered than something to be avoided.

A key element in raising expectations is to equip people with experiences, tips, resources and role models to aid the change. This enhances their ability level in the particular behavior. Rick did this with Stephan. As Rick showed Stephan, while micromanagement is not very effective, its opposite—abandoning your team—can backfire as well. By listening to the call with the Ten Zero team, asking lots of questions, and providing very specific feedback and guidance on what to do, Rick was able to raise Stephan's level of expectation that he could lead at a senior level.

Raising expectations by explaining how to do something or cheerleading along the way are often what most managers and coaches default to when coaching others. While certainly an important part, the best time to get into expectation building is when people explicitly ask for it, not simply off the bat. We call this the "Help Hotline" because people need to want and solicit help before truly listening to any specific advice on how to tackle an issue.

When Stephan asked Rick, "What is the right question to ask Nytasha?" he was truly ready to hear advice. The same was true when Ivan asked Rick for his opinion on what to do to encourage more debate and not shut down discussions. From our experience, all the other factors of our model – Realization, Incentive, Pressure – ought to be lined up in some way before managers get into the nitty-gritty of building Expectation (confidence and ability).

Additionally, micromanagement is a very common issue our coaching clients deal with. Stephan's character was born out of our observations that many of our high-performing, micro-managing clients were also dealing with 'imposter syndrome' in some way due to their race, gender, age, or some other factor that placed them in the minority. We acknowledge that there are real constraints, stereotypes and structural barriers that some people face in the workplace. Some may say that Stephan, as a black man, was over-reacting in his zeal to be perfect, but he was still reacting to the reality that there is a potentially heightened scrutiny over his performance and behavior. Nevertheless, everyone must take ownership over what they can control. That's precisely what Stephan did with Annie through role-playing future scenarios to prepare her mentally and re-frame situations that typically cause her anxiety. Stephan, himself, has to work on shedding some habits he has relied on to get him to where he is now.

A key component is to help people feel a sense of accomplishment and mastery in the issue they're working on or within a similar issue. The positive feedback Rick gave Ivan about how he acted in the town hall is a good example of this. Rick was able to point to that and say, "You're doing it already," and just encourage him to build upon that. We notice in our work with senior executives that the use of reinforcement and positive encouragement is grossly under-leveraged. Just because someone has "made it" to the senior ranks of an organization does not mean they stop benefitting from the power of positive reinforcement that shapes the right behavior and encourages them to keep doing that which is already working for them (or to sustain a recent improvement).

When we coach executives to stretch themselves or change a behavior, and they are already very competent in a number of related or adjacent areas, we leverage their confidence and competence in those areas to help transfer the skills onto the new behavior or approach. Doing so makes it seem less intimidating to try something new because, in fact, they have successfully done something similar before!

Lastly, Arthur's entitled actions are a more extreme example of the various things some Millennials do that tend to frustrate their bosses and older colleagues. We'll dive into his character a little bit more, along with

Betsy's, in the next chapter. For now, we want to say that, while we hear many complaints about Millennials, the issues raised are not much different from what is said with every new incoming generation of leaders. At the end of the day, leaders have to control what they can control. They have a responsibility to lead and work with people, despite their quirks and idiosyncrasies.

BELOW ARE SOME TIPS TO HELP BUILD THE EXPECTATION LEVEL (THE CONFIDENCE AND ABILITY) OF YOUR COACHEES.

- Help them reflect on similar situations where they were previously successful. When people feel low in confidence to make a change, they often get stuck, focusing on their gaps, weaknesses, and reasons why they can't make the change. Redirecting that focus to similar or related successes not only reinforces the success mindset, but also inspires confidence by helping them realize they have overcome similar doubts in the past.

- Provide some "how to" advice to give them the confidence to get started. Be sure to avoid telling them how to do everything though, as this reduces their personal ownership of the success. Wait to provide this advice until the coachee actually wants it (they don't think they have the answer).

- Utilize new job assignments, coupled with times of reflection, to promote new behaviors. For example, you can assign a new project, client or task to a coachee then periodically explore what they are learning or doing differently as a result of this experience. The literature is very clear that on the job learning, coupled with focused reflection, is the most impactful form of learning; far more so than attending courses.

- If an individual's skill and confidence to accomplish a task are low, we recommend prioritizing ability building efforts over confidence building efforts. More skill-building and less cheerleading is the way to approach the early phase of enhancing expectation for most people.

- Individuals who are low in expectation can also learn vicariously by simply watching a role model or mentor display the desired behaviors. This can be a powerful teaching tool. They can replicate then learn to modify the behavior or skill they watch others do well.

- Identify specific barriers inhibiting your coachee from making the desired change. Ask questions and provide advice on how to address any organizational barriers (getting support from a manager, finding a mentor with the skills your coachee wants to improve) or personal barriers (how to proactively access tools to improve skills in the identified area, how to improve one's "self-talk" to boost confidence when things get tough).

- Positive encouragement via direct statements isn't the most sophisticated tool in the toolkit, but it does work! Telling them "I have faith in you" or "You've got this" and "It will all work out, just give it a go" may seem like platitudes, but these kind of cheerleading moments – when combined with other coaching skills – increase confidence (and thus expectation) and motivation. Just be sure they have the tools and skills to achieve basic levels of proficiency at the onset. Don't tell someone who will fail or is failing that they "got this".

- At one point in the preceding chapter, Ivan asks Rick for advice on how to be more effective with Stephan and Tony. Although we have cautioned not to provide advice too soon, once someone is asking for it, they have invited you to do so once you have a good understanding of the issues. This is a perfect time to pivot to providing guidance, advice, and direction.

- When Stephan talks about his challenges in letting go with Ten Zero, he is actually concerned about two things; First, that others on the team won't be able to service the client as effectively as he does; Second, that he is not adding sufficient value to justify stepping away from the account management, creating reputational risk for him.

  We often see our coachees default to doing what they are already good at rather than fumbling along with a new behavior that doesn't come as naturally to them (delegating or thinking more strategically). Exploring these concerns, and mitigating the downside risk, will play a critical role in building your coachee's confidence.

- Finally, ability- and confidence-building takes time. Don't expect one conversation to be sufficient to change a lifetime of behavioral habits. We have found that scheduling regular follow-up meetings to discuss behavior change efforts promotes ongoing dialogue and continuity. In addition, it can be very useful to identify "homework assignments" and "reflection questions" for your coachee to work on in between coaching discussions to promote ongoing skill building. Tracking behavioral progress not only illustrates what's working, but also further contributes to confidence as they expand their ability to sustain the change across situations and over time.

REFLECTION QUESTIONS

1. *Expectation is about having both the confidence to take the desired action as well as the ability. Stephan appears to be relatively low in both confidence and ability to empower Nytasha effectively. If you were coaching Stephan, would you prioritize addressing his confidence or his ability first? Why?*

2. One of the biggest mistakes coaches make is addressing Expectation too soon, which tends to be ineffective. For example, Rick providing Stephan with articles represents an attempt to build his ability in the area prematurely. Why do you think prematurely building ability and confidence can be a well-intended but ultimately misguided effort? How can you tell if the time is "right" to provide "how to" advice?

3. At one point in their coaching session, Rick asks Stephan to play back his understanding of how to empower Nytasha differently. This is often an effective technique when building new skills. People may seem like they understand your message, but may not understand it as well as you think. When assessing another's understanding, why do you think open-ended questions would be more informative than a simple yes or no question? On what specific skills should you assess your coachee's comprehension?

4. Stephan indicates that one factor reducing his confidence in being willing and able to empower his team is the repercussions if meetings don't go well (Bets will be looking for "skulls to crack"). It is useful to explore what associated risks people perceive with making behavior changes, as this both highlights their incentives as well as identifies potential steps the coach or the manager can take to "safety net" the coachee. What perceived risks are holding your coachee back from making a specific change?

5. When Stephan begins to coach Annie on her presentation style, he is addressing her expectation level by providing her with feedback and public speaking tips. What does it say about Annie's levels of

Realization, Incentive and Pressure that she is so apparently open to his guidance? How would you coach Stephan to assess Annie's Realization, Incentive and Pressure to ensure he isn't giving her guidance before she is ready to hear it? Do you think providing guidance to build expectation then assessing one's reaction is a useful way to assess Realization, Incentive and Pressure?

6. *Annie clearly could enhance her public speaking skills. However, through Stephan's coaching of Annie, he also learns that she lacks some self-confidence due to racial and gender identity concerns, which are very private insecurities. What specific behaviors enabled Stephan to get Annie to discuss these confidence challenges so openly with him? How can you uncover and support some of the unspoken fears and concerns that your coachee might struggle with?*

CHAPTER SIX

HEADWINDS AND TAILWINDS

"**Fisher,** you feeling ready?" Stephan greets Rick as he walks through the door of Karpos's headquarters.

Rick feels his chest tightly constrict. "Hold on, is the Ten Zero meeting today? I thought it was Thursday?"

"Oh no," Stephan says, shaking his head seriously. "We're about to get on a video conference with them in five minutes. It was scheduled for Tuesday, not Thursday."

"Crap!" Rick blurts out. "Crap, I need to grab some things from my desk."

Suddenly, Betsy's voice appears behind Rick's ear. "Fisher, you do know what day it is, right?"

"Betsy!" Rick stiffens up. "I didn't see you walk up. Yes, it is Tuesday. I knew that. I just didn't get the date right—"

"Relax, Fisher," Betsy starts laughing. "We've been seeing you all wound up and stressed over this meeting for weeks now, so Stephan and I came up with this idea five minutes ago to prank you. The meeting is on Thursday."

Stephan interjects, "I'll take the fall for this one. It was my idea, Fisher, not Betsy's. I roped her into it."

Betsy smiles and turns around, "I've got to get back to work. I'll let you two hash this out."

"Jeez, Stephan," Rick exhales, slumping his shoulders. "You definitely got my heart racing. These kind of surprises are definitely *not* what my doctor recommended!"

Stephan jabs Rick lightly in the shoulder, "Think of it as good cardio exercise. We do have a meeting coming up soon though. Annie is presenting."

"So," Rick says, as he starts to walk towards his office, gesturing for Stephan to follow him. "This is actually happening? Will she be okay in front of a client?"

"We'll find out in the next 30 minutes. She's been preparing all weekend for this and emailing me questions."

"Excuse me?" Arthur knocks on the door of Rick's office, where Stephan and Rick are chatting. "I heard from Annie that she has a chance to be at the Ten Zero meeting and she's presenting in front of you?"

"Yes, we're excited to hear what she has to say," Stephan says.

"I forgot to say," Rick chimes in, "thanks for giving us the idea of having an analyst there at the meeting. We wouldn't have thought of it if it weren't for you."

"Of course...." Arthur says, trying to think of what to say. "I was actually thinking that I would be—"

Stephan butts in, "Before I forget, Arthur, are you done with the solar pool heating report yet?"

"Oh, no. I'm having issues with our system, but I'll figure it out and get it to you tomorrow at the latest."

"I did remind you on Friday that it was due this morning right? We're having a meeting to discuss pool heating tomorrow morning and I was counting on having today to review it."

"Right, I'll get it to you by end of day today," Arthur replies and quickly switches topics. "I actually was wondering why Annie got this opportunity and I didn't when it was my idea in the first place."

"Arthur," Stephan says, "Why don't you come in, have a seat and close the door?"

Arthur walks over and plops down on the chair. Crossing his legs at a wide angle, he turns to face Stephan, who says, "We'll be more than happy to discuss an opportunity for you to be in the same room with a client if the stars align. But it's hard for me to think about that at this juncture when I feel you haven't met basic requirements."

"What do you mean?"

"Turning things in on time, for one."

Arthur adjusts his collar and says, "Of course I've got to get better at that, but you never have a problem with what I turn in, right?"

"No, it's usually quite good."

"And you have no problem with my presentation skills?"

"No, you're great, in fact."

"So," Arthur cocks his head and replies, "I guess I don't understand. I always do good work, but I'm not great on deadlines. That's just who I am. But obviously," he adds, "I wouldn't be late for a report that had a very important deadline like a Ten Zero meeting. I turned in the New Mexico report on time a few weeks ago, remember?"

"Arthur," Stephan replies firmly. "That was the exception not the norm. Plus, when people provide you feedback on your drafts, you dismiss a lot of it."

"That's because I think a lot of the feedback is subjective and not objective. Look, I'm a good writer. I know how to write—"

Rick, who has been replying to emails, interjects, "But if you're going to reject someone's feedback, Arthur, you have to tell them why. You owe them an explanation."

"All right, I can do that. I have been doing that in some cases."

Stephan goes on, "It's also little things here and there that add up, Arthur. When you were working on that poly panels report, you missed that deadline. When I told you we needed it soon, you still left early anyways."

"My hot yoga class is always at 5:30, and I can't change that schedule," Arthur replied.

Rick stands up and fiddles with his cuff links. "I think Stephan and I are both due to Betsy's office for Annie's presentation in fifteen minutes, and I need to finish typing this last email in quiet."

Stephan gestures for Arthur to come with him as they exit Rick's office. Rick exhales and is thankful to have some quiet.

❖ ❖ ❖ ❖ ❖

A few minutes before the meeting, Rick heads down the hallway to Betsy's office. He wants to chat with her about the Arizona campaign before the whole troop shows up.

He knocks on her door and Betsy gestures for him to come in. Before he even opens his mouth, she asks, "I hear that the Chasers are in the Spring Championship! That's this Friday, right?"

Rick grins, "Yes, they are. Great recall! Jo had to remind me last week when it was. She did the whole, 'Dad, can't you read? The schedule's on the wall.'"

Betsy smiles and lifts a cup of coffee, "That sounds about right. When my kids were Jo's age, they wanted to keep conversations with us as minimal as possible. Of course they spent hours on the phone with their friends though."

"I don't even think Jo talks over the phone these days," Rick shakes his head. "Now it's all, Snapchat or Instagram stories. The only time she uses the call button on her phone is for me, I think."

"Speaking of," Betsy changes the topic. "I didn't get a ton of context for this presentation we're about to have. Stephan told me that we're having one of our analysts come and present before we commence our prep meeting for Ten Zero?"

"Yes, her name is Annie. Have you met her yet? She started with the other analyst. They're both quite sharp Millennials. Although, one's a bit more colorful than the other, shall we say?"

"Are you referring to Arthur? He introduced himself to me after the town hall," Betsy replies. "I don't think I've formally met Annie, although I have seen her around." She pauses then continues, "I don't understand why we think she should be in the Ten Zero meeting? It's going to look odd to have all these senior people in the room and… a young analyst. People may start asking questions about why she got this opportunity while others didn't."

Rick replies, "Don't ask me. Stephan is the one who seems to think highly of her, and I say, why not. It's only fifteen minutes of our time. Maybe we'll learn something from her presentation."

"Sure, but this is such an important meeting. We can't make any mistakes," Betsy says emphatically. "It'll be our first big services contract. It's not just about the $5 million. It's about the investor call next week too. They want to see evidence that our strategy is paying off. If it goes well, they could agree to be featured in our Arizona campaign, which would be huge."

At that moment Ivan, Stephan and Annie walk in.

"So here's the troop," Betsy says, rising out of her seat to greet everyone, starting with Annie. "Annie, it's a pleasure to finally meet you."

Stephan smiles, "Bets, is this is your first time formally meeting her? Well, this will not be your first time encountering her work. She was the brains behind the Arizona solar trends report we put out, as well as some of the strategy behind the Arizona and the Florida services campaign too. You've probably read her writing many times by now."

"Ah," Betsy lights up, "I liked that report. I got a handful of replies from various CEOs after I sent that out. The Florida campaign, I thought, was quite well done too."

"Whoa," Rick jokes, holding up his watch, "Annie's been working a little over a month and already she has received more compliments than I've ever gotten from Betsy!"

Ivan joins in, smiling, "Don't flatter yourself, Fisher. When have you ever received a compliment from Bets?"

"Ouch," Rick laughs and rejoins, "Ivan, your head is so big you probably think everyone's complimenting you every day."

"All right, settle down boys," Betsy looks at them with raised eyebrows and uses a more serious tone.

"Before we get started," she says, "tell me, Annie, since we haven't formally met—which is my fault since I've been very busy, I really do try and sit down all new hires within a month of them starting - what made you decide to join our firm?"

Annie freezes as all the eyes in the room turn towards her. Betsy sits behind her desk. Ivan and Rick sit next to each other on a three-seat lounge chair, with a coffee table in front of them. Stephan stands, leaning next to a chair that has his jacket placed upon it. There are a few empty chairs next to his. Annie takes a deep breath and focuses her gaze on the person addressing her, Betsy in this case, as Stephan advised.

"I've always been interested in solar energy," she starts saying. "I studied Environmental Science in college and knew, after various internships and my first job, that I wanted to focus on data, because I could see that data informs basically every important decision a business makes. So, um, I took a few courses on data science, which is how I'm here, doing this job."

Betsy nods, "But why Karpos? Are you from San Diego?"

"Actually, my whole family moved to San Diego recently from the suburbs near Detroit. I liked Karpos for a lot of reasons," Annie says.

"Go on," Betsy nods.

"Well, I love your company's purpose to provide renewable energy and reduce carbon emissions. That aligns with my college studies. I felt you have high-quality products, and I liked the business opportunities you are exploring," Annie says, pausing before continuing. "I also appreciated the fact that it was led by a female CEO. Most of the companies that I was talking to were led by men."

Betsy lets out a bark of laughter, "That's an understatement if I ever heard one. I've got some stories to share, Annie, if we ever have the time. Starting a solar company in 1999 will teach you a few things."

Stephan chimes in, "Bets, come out to one of our happy hours sometime. We haven't seen you at the last few. Tell your stories then."

"I know, I will, but let's not delay Annie any longer," Betsy says, re-focusing the room.

"Oh wait," Stephan pipes up. "Could we wait a bit longer? I'd like Nytasha to be here for this. I forgot to tell her about Annie's presentation. I think it'll be useful for her to get up to speed on what Annie is saying."

"Is she joining the prep meeting after this?" Betsy asks.

"Yes, she was on the invite because she's been in many of the discussions with Ten Zero, so she'll have some insights to share," Stephan replies. "And I can see Rick staring at me out of the corner of my eye; I am also trying to transition that account to her so I'm not their point-person anymore."

"Is that so?" Betsy says, looking at Rick then Stephan. "Well I'm glad to hear that. That's the right thing to do especially now that you're in a regional role. Good coaching, Rick."

"Thanks, Bets," Rick says. "Actually, while we're waiting for Nytasha, can we talk quickly about the Arizona marketing campaign? I think it may make more sense for you to call Ten Zero's VP of Marketing about featuring them in some of the promos. But we do need to discuss the timing of that ask…"

As they continue to discuss various logistics, Annie's mind starts to wander and think of how weird it is that she is standing here, in this room, about to give this presentation with the CEO of her company as her audience. She can almost see Arthur standing in the left corner of the room, staring at her in mock admiration ("how did you get *that* invite?" he asked her when she told him about this). She tries to focus on the moment and starts to feel a bit dizzy.

She recalls Stephan's reassurance that her co-workers speak highly of her. She also thinks of her family, with whom she has rehearsed this presentation multiple times over the weekend. They don't quite understand her job, and she has tried to explain to them how this job aligned with her values and passion for renewable energy, as well as her interest and skills in data analytics, but to little avail. She thought this presentation might be a way to clarify what she does.

However, there was no light-bulb moment for any of them, but it didn't go badly either. "What do you mean by 'data'?" her mom asked, but Annie couldn't explain it any better. Nevertheless, they gave her tips on where she should place her hands when she talked, pointed out when she was too quiet and needed to speak up and told her at the end that she sounded impressive and smart. Even though they couldn't digest the content of the presentation, they tried hard to help, and for that, she was grateful.

"Nytasha's here. Let's get started. Annie?"

The faces of her family recede into the background and the faces in front of her come into full visibility. "Yes, I'll start," she says, firmly.

She begins her presentation, starting first with a quick news story and connecting that to a few industry trends nationally then locally within Arizona. Her intonation is well timed and deliberate, as she emphasizes certain key words over others and takes pain to articulate every syllable. She pauses between important sentences, instead of filling them with "um's" as she did in her previous presentations. As she goes on, her volume increases and she begins to paint a picture of the opportunities and risks of investing in solar in Arizona, concluding with a strong case of what Karpos is doing to take advantage of those opportunities and mitigate those risks. After she finishes the last word of her presentation, she takes a breath and looks at the faces in front her, expectantly.

"Brava, Annie," Betsy says, taking off her glasses, smiling. Next to her, she sees Stephan, nodding proudly.

❖ ❖ ❖ ❖ ❖

After the group dispersed from the prep meeting, Rick decided to take a walk outside and grab some fresh air. He isn't particularly hungry, and his mind feels cloudy with the buzz of several thoughts that he wants to collect and organize.

He thinks about how well Annie's presentation went. He had totally written her off as someone who'd always play support and never take center stage, much less in front of senior leaders. She has improved dramatically since the last time he heard her present on that conference call. "She must have really absorbed Stephan's advice and tips. Arthur, on the other hand, couldn't have been more defensive when Stephan gave him feedback. He delivers good work, but as the company grows, we need people, especially in Arthur's role, willing and flexible enough to adapt to whatever is asked of them. Arthur probably has low natural inclination, but there has to be a way to heighten his "ripeness" for change. How long should he be given before deciding he isn't a fit for Karpos?" Rick wonders.

As he enters a local park near the office, his thoughts take a different turn.

Nytasha brought up some great insights about Ten Zero during the prep meeting, and Stephan did not interrupt her or try to jump in at the end of her sentences. Rick is glad that Stephan is including her in more strategic meetings.

"It's about time. Also, Ivan was actually pretty good at listening and building off what people said instead of just charging in with what he's been planning on saying all along. Even Bets, who these days is usually as unsentimental as a rock, opened up a bit more with Annie around," recalls Rick. "I wonder how to encourage this side of her. It's much more inspiring than her typical stone-faced exterior," he reflects to himself.

"A few months ago, I would've completely ignored that question and said that's beyond my pay grade," Rick smiles to himself as he thinks about how much of an impact his conversations with Erin have had. "I'm more reflective and less reactive, and actually inclined to think about what I can take responsibility for. Maybe I can try again with Bets.

"But is the juice worth the squeeze?" he thinks as he kicks a pebble down the pathway. "If I bring up my observations with Bets and things go badly, I'm screwed. If I do and they go well, then both she and Karpos benefits, but do I benefit too? What's my upside?

"The truth is," he ruminates, "that it is hard to motivate my sales team, especially those who are based in San Diego, in a high-pressure, low-morale office environment. The impact that Bets is having on others is starting to affect my team's performance and me.

"I could leave Karpos, of course. That's one option. But, I've invested five years into this company, and Karpos is now at a turning point. If I can help turn this ship around, not only would it be a meaningful success, it would also be huge for my career. Plenty of companies are in Karpos's situation as a solid industry player, but many are also fading slowly and trying to pivot from manufacturing to services.

"Which brings me back to Bets. What did Erin say? 'Don't make it about whose perceptions are objectively right. Make it about 'acknowledging people's perceptions, since she has to lead these people anyways.' How is that supposed to work exactly?"

His stomach begins to rumble and Rick turns back towards the office.

He adjusts his route so that he can walk past the food truck where Stephan and he get tacos. After grabbing a few to go, he walks into the office and bumps straight into Betsy.

"Fisher," she says. "I'm actually not feeling terrible about this meeting on Thursday. How about you?"

"You know," he replies. "I'm pleased that we are coming together as a team. Of course, we'll try to anticipate all the possible reactions that Ten Zero's team can have, but ultimately, I feel confident that we can respond to whatever they throw at us."

"Very optimistic of you," she says. "Walk with me to my office for a second, will you?"

When she closes the door, she turns to Rick and says, "I just want to say again that I am pleased with how much better you and Ivan are working together. This is a huge improvement from even a few months ago. I asked Ivan about it after the meeting we just had, and you may be surprised to hear he actually credited you for catalyzing this change in your dynamic."

Rick stifles his slight surprise. "Well yes, I think it took me a while, but I finally started seeing and treating him as a member of the team. And you have always said that you don't let your teammates sink or swim on their own."

"You still remember that from the office tour I gave you on your first day?" Betsy smiles. "When I pointed to our core values?"

"Oh yes," Rick nods. "Because I think that's how you, and many of us here, try to live. You helped me learn the ropes on some of the more technical stuff around solar in my first year. And Stephan, well, he went out of his way to help Annie with that presentation."

"Speaking of Stephan," she says. "I was pleasantly surprised to see him bringing Nytasha into the meeting, who had some smart things to say. I admit I was a bit worried when you promoted him over some others with more experience, but now I see that he's really taking to the management part of the role. He gets that it's more than just hitting his numbers."

"Yeah," Rick chuckles. "You don't want to know how long and hard we had to work to get there. It was frustrating in the beginning, but I do feel he's on the right track now.

"Honestly," he adds, "this whole process has been a bit of a lesson in learning that people can change—even those who I initially write off—so long as the right conditions are in place. And I'm learning what I can do to help make that happen."

"You are becoming a great leader, Fisher," Betsy replies. "Which is partly why I wanted to talk to you.

"Have a seat," she continues, as she sits down behind her desk, "I have some news for you."

She takes a breath and clasps her hands together. "I'm going to retire in the next two years or so. I've told the board and a few others, but you're the first person on the executive team. I'm going to tell the others tomorrow, so keep this to yourself when you leave this room."

"Wow," Rick replies, stunned as he shuffles into his chair. "I didn't quite see this coming. I guess I never pictured you as someone who... retired."

"I know, this is my baby," she says, sighing. "And I've worked myself to the bone to get this going and running and steady. Trust me, it was a long and hard decision to make, but I think it's the right move for me and perhaps for Karpos as well."

"Can I ask why you are telling me first?"

"Because," Betsy explains, with a wistful look in her eyes, "we're going through so much change now, and we're going to go through even more change when I'm gone. I want to make sure that we're aligned on the change we want to happen."

"Oh, are you asking me for my thoughts?" Rick replied a bit surprised.

"Yes."

"In terms of strategy," Rick thinks quickly, "I do think we are making the right move with investing in servicing and not just manufacturing, given the trends. And I think Ivan is starting to gel a bit better with Karpos's folks."

"I wanted to ask you more about that," she interjects. "How did your relationship turn around so fast?"

Rick hesitates. Should he tell her about Erin and the whole story? He has never been quite this open and vulnerable with Betsy, but he has a feeling that maybe now is the time to do it and perhaps it will help her open up as well.

He starts from the beginning with how he started talking to Erin the night that he was supposed to call Ivan. He walks Betsy through how Erin helped him work with Ivan.

"And," he adds quickly, "she was very helpful in helping me coach Stephan to let go of micromanaging the way he was used to."

"This Coach Erin sounds very interesting; kind of like a coach of coaches," Betsy says, as Rick wraps up his stories. She leans back in a chair and twirls a pen around her fingers.

"Yes, she's a character," he responds, nodding his head. "I was just out for a walk during lunch-time reflecting on all the things I've been learning and taking stock. I used to be someone who wrote people off or blamed others more easily when things weren't going well. Not to sound cheesy here—"

"This is turning into a Lifetime movie," Betsy chuckles, "but go on."

"I know," Rick says, feeling a bit flushed. "I guess I'd say that she's helped me take more responsibility for what I can control, as well become a bit more empathetic and attuned to where others are coming from and what they need to get from A to B. It's not enough to just direct or instruct people to produce the change you want, which was what I was initially doing with Stephan. You have to dig into their incentives, belief systems, and habits and work with them."

"That sounds like a lot of work," Betsy observes. "Can't people just be adults and find it within themselves to get on with the program? Why all this extra coaching and managing?"

"It is not easy and is a lot of work," Rick nods. "I see your point and agree with you in simple situations. I don't need 'coaching' on how to get out of bed every morning to show up to work. I do that myself. But, there are some areas that are more complex. I think the issue is that people aren't robots. We're human and can't just be programmed to change immediately. Thus, things are a little messy sometimes."

Betsy takes a moment to absorb all of this and responds, "So based on what you've learned, what are your thoughts on how should I go about getting people ready for change, both now and five years from now?"

Rick is surprised and can't believe she's asking him for advice! He ends up blurting out, "Have you been noticing how the morale feels in the office lately? Take the town hall last week. What was your read on how people were behaving or engaged?"

Betsy looks at him in the eyes. "Fisher, just say it. What's with these leading questions?"

"I mean, you've been noticing it yourself," he replies, trying to come up with the right words. "You talked about how you've been noticing people are leaving before five o'clock in recent months.

"And," he decides to keep going, maintaining eye contact, "during the town hall, I couldn't help but notice that many people dialed in rather than attend. And, those who were there, except for senior management, were tuned out. They were either on their phones or just slouched on their chairs, staring into space."

Betsy replies, "I did notice that and I have been noticing it. That's why I've been trying to raise the level of urgency a bit more, push harder, and demand more. That is my reaction when I sense people getting lazy and apathetic around here."

"I know you think that we need new blood, which might be true," he says, measuring his words carefully and making eye contact with her again. "But maybe a slightly different tone from the top would help too. What I learned from coaching Stephan is that sometimes even when people realize they need to change, have an incentive to do so, and feel the pressure to do so, it still may not be enough.

"People need to feel confident that they can pull off the change required of them. It's the Expectation factor. That's the missing element here, I feel. People need to feel equipped with the right resources, training and guidance as well as to feel that their jobs aren't on the line if they make a mistake."

"What do you mean?" Betsy says, with an edge in her voice as she scrutinizes him through her glasses.

Rick sits back in his chair and holds up one hand. "Okay so, just to give you an example, your tone right there makes me feel like I should just shut up and not say anymore."

Betsy rolls her eyes, "That's not my fault. That's on you for feeling like that. That's not what I intended at all. I just wanted clarification."

"I'm sure that's what you intended," Rick says, relaxing his body language and recalling Erin's advice about objective and subjective perceptions. "All I'm saying is that this is how I feel. I feel a bit intimidated and discouraged from contributing more or saying anything at all. And if I feel this way, I imagine others in the organization feel it at least as much as I do."

"Okay, but why is that something I should work on? Maybe you should work on feeling less intimidated," Betsy responds sharply.

"You know," she continues, "if I ever treated feeling intimidated by other people as a reason not to raise my voice in a meeting or not to pursue an opportunity, I would not be here now. Believe me, I've had to fight past some really tough and demanding people to get to where I am. I had to get tough myself and develop a thick skin.

"Which is why," she finishes, "I have high standards for people, and can sometimes be mistaken as being too 'intimidating' or 'demanding.' Perhaps some people here just aren't used to getting this type of leadership from a woman."

Rick quickly replies, "Oh, I'm sure that is the case for some people. And, I get that you have plenty of legitimate reasons for doing what you do. In fact, one of the reasons why so many people here, including me, respect you is because of what you've been able to accomplish despite the odds."

He takes a breath and adds, "Betsy, I'm not here to judge your motivations or weigh in on who's right or wrong at all. That's not my place. All I'm pointing out is that I feel, in the past few years, especially as Karpos has had to weather some turbulence, like you've gotten tougher and, quite frankly, scarier.

"This may just be my perception, but it is certainly real in its effects on people. Doesn't that make your job harder?"

"Yeah, I guess it does," Betsy admits. "I feel people are shrinking from me recently, instead of engaging with me."

"So, unless you're going to fire everyone tomorrow, I think you probably have to work with this perception, instead of outright dismissing it, which is not what I'm saying you are doing at all, but…"

"Let's be concrete here," she cuts him off. "What exactly are you suggesting I do? I do actually want to know, because I want to be intentional in what I do and how I act in the next two years as I transition out. If there is something I can do, without compromising who I am, to be a better leader, I want to know."

Rick is rather surprised by this turn in the conversation. This is not what he expected at all when he bumped into Betsy at the door. Her looming retirement seems to be opening up a different side of her.

"Bets," he says, clearing his throat, "I just want to make clear that I totally respect who you are – your toughness, your determination, your intelligence—these are the strengths that keep this company going and you shouldn't change that."

"Thanks, but no need to flatter me. I get it, Fisher."

"I guess I'm saying that I don't *want* you to change who you are; just adapt a few behaviors and become a bit more mindful as to how people might feel. Be a bit more sensitive and inspirational, in other words."

Betsy sits back into her chair, her hand on her chin, thinking. She feels the urge to argue back, but calms herself down instead. Ultimately, when she does retire from Karpos, all that is left besides its IP, products and capital are its people. She wants to be sure that the people whom she entrusts to take over will not fall apart and fail. So, she concludes the need to be more thoughtful about her impact on the workforce.

Finally, she speaks, "You know I used to be a bit more feelings-oriented, but starting and running this company, especially in recent years, has changed me. Even my husband has said so. I guess I have to tap into my old self a bit more."

"Actually," Rick says, "and I really want to say this. I see that side of you from time to time, especially when I first started. During my second week at Karpos, you asked me how Jo was dealing with her transition to middle school. She was actually having a hard time because we had just moved school districts, and you asking meant a lot. I was surprised you even remembered that small detail from our interviews."

"Yes, I try to remember all these things. As someone who's tried really hard to balance my life outside of work and my life at work, I understand."

"And the fact that you asked me made me think Karpos is a good place to build a career," Rick replies. "You are great at remembering birthdays and treating us like we are people, not just employees. All that's needed is to extend that attitude and consider that we are people when we work too, if that makes sense."

Betsy's phone starts ringing. She looks at her cell phone briefly and looks up at Rick, "I don't mean to be rude, but this is a call I can't miss, unfortunately. Let's continue this conversation another time. You've given me a lot of food for thought and I want some time to think over what you said. Perhaps we can get dinner and get into more concrete details."

"So I'm not fired?" Rick laughs, a bit nervously.

Betsy smiles. "You're not. In fact, I'm glad we're talking because I am thinking about my successor, and whoever that person is will need to be fairly adaptable and think along the same lines you do. But, I do need to take this call. Thanks for your candor, Fisher."

Rick jumps up from his seat. "Sure thing. Talk to you later."

As he closes the door, Rick pauses for a moment to let sink in what just happened. He shakes his head as if to wake up from a dream and walks towards the men's room so he can wash his face.

His phone buzzes with a text from Jo, "Softball practice canceled today due to rain ☹. We're just going to warm up longer before the championship on fri."

Rick is bummed there will be no meeting with Erin today. He has so much to tell her. But, he is confident she would say, "Good job, Rick."

TAKEAWAYS AND TIPS:

Out of all the characters in the book, Ivan and Arthur are probably the most resistant to change, exhibiting low levels of natural inclination. People with low natural inclination may very be talented and successful, but believe their abilities are fixed traits. They feel that their success "naturally" results from their strengths and their weaknesses are, more or less, just a part of who they are, making them unable to veer outside of their behavioral comfort zone.

This is illustrated in remarks, such as "this is who I am" and in their defensiveness around feedback. Arthur explains away feedback about the tardiness of his assignments as being a character flaw of his. He also dismisses the feedback he receives on his reports. People with low natural inclination are unlikely to seek out feedback or stretch assignments that demand the development of new skills. They don't believe they are capable of deep change and simply look to play to their existing strengths as much as possible.

As Erin mentions, you can think of having low natural inclination as having a headwind. It makes the behavioral change journey more difficult, but not impossible. Ivan's attitude was very similar to Arthur's in the beginning of the book, but through becoming "ripened" on other factors – Incentive and Pressure – he eventually started to deploy new behaviors.

Having high natural inclination – like Annie or Rick – acts as a tailwind, accelerating the pace of change. Instead of a "fixed mindset," Annie and Rick exhibit a "growth mindset" (the esteemed social psychologist Carol Dweck has devoted much of her career to exploring growth vs. fixed mindsets and has reviewed much of her research in her book *Mindset*). People with a growth mindset believe that their most basic abilities can be developed through curiosity, dedication, and hard work. In other words, while natural talent matters to them, they believe that is just a starting point. People with high natural inclination are generally committed to self-improvement, open to new experiences, and learning new things or skills. Thus, they are generally more open to coaching and require less time invested in exploring the various stages of the RIPEN model. When managers think of their coaching successes, they are likely reflecting on people who possessed high Natural Inclination.

In the case of Annie, although she saw herself as someone who is 'bad at public speaking,' she didn't let that belief prevent her efforts to improve. Over a matter of days, she worked hard to absorb Stephan's feedback. In the end, she truly stepped up to the plate. She represents the *other* type of Millennial that is under-represented in the discussions of Millennials. Yes, some are entitled, like Arthur, and may have lower levels of natural inclination, but not all Millennials should be lumped into the same category.

As one of our insightful clients said during a training program a while back, "Millennial is a mindset, not an age." Point taken! Overgeneralizing an age-cohort doesn't help leaders know how to handle the people challenges on their team. Sure, understanding some general themes about any given population can be helpful, but we know from the emerging research and our own practical experience across client organizations that all employees – across all age demographics – want useful feedback and coaching from their boss that helps them grow and develop. That's why we believe focusing on the "basics" of being an effective coach, rather than blaming the employee for being difficult, hard to motivate, or born during a certain generation is the best approach to take if you want to be a highly effective leader.

We have seen Rick, Ivan, Stephan and even Annie through much of their journeys, and in this chapter, we start to see the beginnings of Betsy's as well. She would probably score a "moderate" on natural inclination. On one hand, she sticks to her guns and is quite stubborn, often attributing responsibility to others. On the other hand, she is open to direct feedback and will adjust if she understands the importance and incentive of doing so.

There seem to be two reasons for her openness to Rick's feedback. One is that that her pending retirement has established the right Pressure and Incentive to adjust her behavior, as she wants to ensure that Karpos's employees will be good stewards of her legacy. The other is that she knows she is capable of doing what Rick is asking for. She alludes to being more sensitive and attuned to people's feelings and perceptions in the past, and must tap into that 'old self' a bit more in order to recalibrate her leadership.

One way to instill confidence and raise expectation is to remind people that what you're asking of them is not a big stretch. It might simply be about tweaking something they are already doing or tapping into a side of themselves that they don't often display, for whatever reason.

IF YOU BELIEVE YOUR COACHEE HAS LOW NATURAL INCLINATION, CONSIDER THE FOLLOWING:

- Natural Inclination is more of a fixed personality style than a task specific attribute. If someone exhibits a great degree of openness to self-development in several areas, but not in another area, don't mistake this with low natural inclination. Instead, this is suggestive that more time and exploration needs to be focused on assessing Realization, Incentive, Pressure and Expectation. Thus, getting a better sense of an individual's track record of personal development is one useful topic to probe in coaching discussions (as well as in hiring interviews). Do they willingly engage in this, or tend to consistently *endure* development experiences because they are required at times?

- Identify behaviors that your coachee has successfully improved upon through their personal growth and development efforts. Not only should this highlight that development is possible for those low in natural inclination, but it also likely highlights what other RIPEN factors were necessary or present that enabled your coachee to make this change. What incentives were powerful? Was there a salient urgency driver? How did they come to learn about the need for development? All of these can be emulated in the current coaching discussion.

- Many development areas are actually a negative consequence of over-using a strength. For example, Bets's results orientation is generally a strength that has served Karpos and her well. When working with those who are low in natural inclination, it can be useful to show how a development area is actually an extension of one's strengths and explore if these strengths can be deployed in a more targeted or thoughtful manner. This avoids having to fundamentally change who one is. In these situations, we tend to ask our coachees questions, such as "In what situations can you enhance the utilization of your strength with no negative repercussions?" and, more importantly, "In what situations should you reduce the utilization of this particular strength?" This approach is particularly helpful for those low in natural inclination, as they tend to find it easier to do less of something they already know how to do versus learn an entirely new skill.

- It is particularly important to emphasize that the changes being made are about behavioral tweaks rather than personality changes when coaching someone low in natural inclination.

- Those with low natural inclination tend to need more direct and frequent feedback, clearer and more significant incentives (often avoidance motivators), clearer urgency drivers, and more time focusing on skill and confidence building. Most can and do make changes, it just requires more consistency and patience from their coaches.

REFLECTION QUESTIONS

1. *In this book, Arthur and Ivan are both characters exhibiting low natural inclination to make changes or accept feedback. In your experience, what personality factors are associated with low natural inclination?*

2. *Most individuals with low natural inclination can ultimately respond well to coaching on specific behavioral changes. However, more emphasis needs to be placed on raising levels of Incentive and Realization. What have you previously done to successfully coach someone who is generally resistant to self-development?*

3. *Not all individuals who are low in natural inclination are able to make the changes as a result of coaching. What signs suggest you should "cut the cord" and no longer invest in someone's development on a specific issue?*

4. *When Rick is speaking with Bets, he indicates that not all coaching discussions require deep deliberation regarding personal accountability, incentives, and confidence. What sort of coaching discussions lend themselves naturally to these deeper conversations, and what sort of coaching topics would benefit from straightforward direction and advice giving?*

5. *Upward coaching is trickier than any other type of coaching because the risks are higher. If it doesn't go well, it can adversely*

impact you and your career. However, the upside can be great as well. Helping your boss address a behavior that is a thorn in your side (like Rick attempted to do with Bets's harsh style) can improve your day-to-day life at work. There is also the potential benefit of your boss trusting you more for being a truth teller and straight shooter, setting you apart from the vast majority of your peers. In our experience, the more senior one gets, the less unvarnished truth one hears from others. Thus, the ability to be effective in upward coaching is a true differentiator in one's career, if done well. What behaviors did Rick do that enabled him to upward-coach Bets effectively?

The crowd erupts. Everyone jumps up from the metal stands.

"Chasers! Chasers! Chasers!" the crowd starts chanting as the girls sprint towards and pile onto the pitcher, who has just struck out the last batter, winning them the game 8-7, and ending a 3-hour softball game that went into extra innings on an unusually hot June day.

After several minutes, Jo emerges from the sweaty, dusty pile and spots her dad in the stands, hooting and hollering like a fool with the rest of the fans. She is too happy to be embarrassed and waves at him vigorously.

Rick, beside himself in joy, waves back at her, only to feel a tap on his shoulder.

"Are you Joanna Fisher's father?"

A pony-tailed, dark-haired woman in sunglasses is standing behind him.

"Uh, yes. I'm Rick Fisher," he replies, unsure who this is.

"I'm Koru," she reaches out her hand to shake it. "I'm a scout for Cal State Chico. I came here to watch Jo play, and I'd like to speak with Jo and you sometime. Here's my card."

Rick takes her card enthusiastically and carefully places it into his wallet. "Oh wow, Jo loves Cal State's softball team. She's been following you guys for a while."

"We've been keeping tabs on her too," Koru replies. "I'm impressed with her performance throughout the playoffs, this game in particular. We'd love to chat more."

They continue to talk for a bit while the Chasers huddle for a post-game debrief in the outfield. Afterwards, the girls return to the dugout to pack up their things. In the corner of her eye, Erin spots Rick approaching the dugout and turns to greet him.

"Congratulations, Erin!"

"Rick, I missed you on Tuesday! How did the client meeting go?"

"Oh, it was fantastic! We're this close to closing a huge, multi-million dollar deal with Ten Zero, including both panels and services. We're trying to expand into Arizona so signing this contract is huge," Rick says enthusiastically.

"Amazing," Erin replies. "And how did the whole team work together?"

"Oh, we were great. Ivan and I worked really well together. He even cracked a few self-deprecating jokes during the meeting. And, Stephan brought in a few junior people, who were great, specifically a younger woman named Annie and a sales manager, Nytasha, whom he's training.

"It's been a pretty high drama week. One of our analysts, Arthur, has been giving us a hard time so we talked with him earlier today and decided that we weren't the right fit for him. He wants a different kind of workplace where he can climb higher, faster, and we want him to be able to master the basics before he can ascend. He's going to stay on for another month so he can have the time to find another gig."

"That's a pity," Erin replies. "I hope he finds a place better suited for him."

"And the big news," Rick says, "is that Betsy and I are scheduled to have dinner early next week. She's looking to retire in the next two years and has basically hinted several times throughout the week that she is thinking of me as her successor."

Erin exclaims, "Wow, how on earth did that happen?"

"She said she's been pretty impressed with my development as a leader and coach, especially in regards to how I've been relating to Ivan and managing Stephan. I told her about your framework, RIPEN, and gave you all the credit, of course."

"Nonsense," Erin smiles. "I have the easy job. You're the one putting in the hard work and actually doing the deed."

They continue to chat a little longer before Jo tugs on Rick's shoulder. "Dad, where are we going to celebrate? Can we bring the whole team?"

"Good idea," he replies. "Let's do Luzzo's?"

Joanna nods, "Yes, perfect. I'll tell everyone."

She steps back and raises her voice so everyone can hear. "My dad and I are inviting everyone out to a celebratory dinner at Luzzo's. Meet us there at 8pm!"

Everyone hollers and cheers. Rick smiles and raises his fist, leading the crowd in one last chant:

"Cha-sers! Cha-sers! Cha-sers!"

RIPEN MODEL: A SUMMARY

Here is a brief overview of our RIPEN model, which can improve coaching outcomes by helping coaches maximize the factors that make people "ready" to be coached. We are providing this summary of the model so all of the concepts are in one easy-to-skim section. Detailed recommendations on how to enhance specific elements of RIPEN are at the end of each chapter. If you want to know more about how to increase your "ripeness" to make a change, you can visit us at www.getripenow.com or if you want to take our RIPEN assessment you can visit https://surveys.avionconsulting.com/ RIPEN.

Although the model is introduced in a linear way, the process of change is rarely so. People move back and forth between each factor, depending on the context. Also, significant improvements can be stymied by a high stress situation, causing people to revert to their instinctive ways of behaving. For example, we once coached a CFO who had received very critical feedback regarding his emotional outbursts and churlishness when he felt decisions were made without sufficiently involving him. Throughout the course of our working together, this leader made great improvements in his composure and proactively building relationships with other members of the executive team. However, on the night before the company's IPO, he had a meltdown

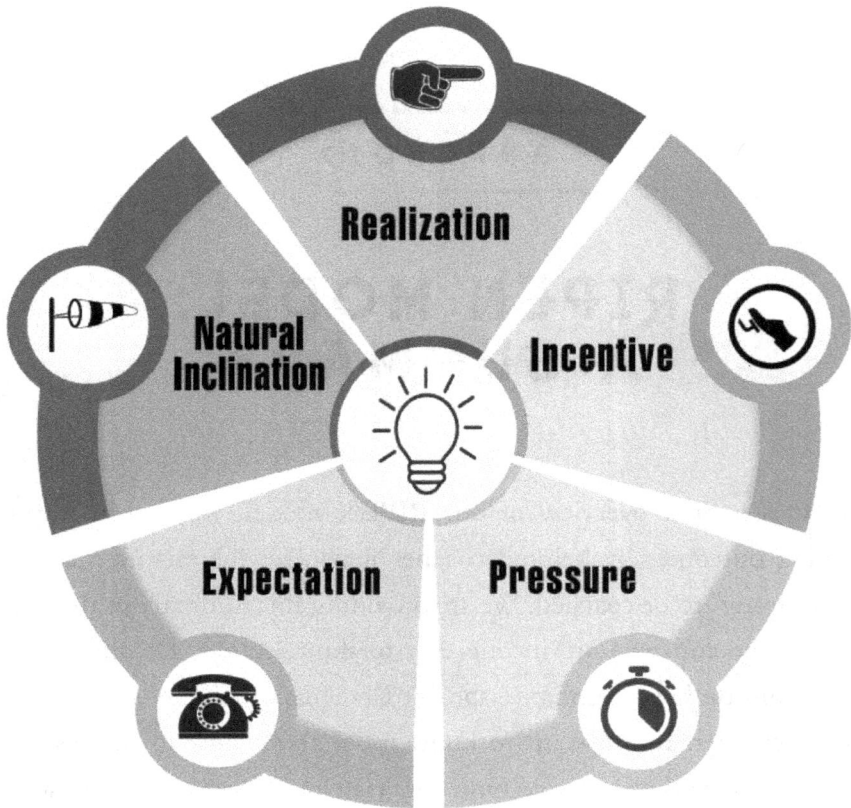

and reverted to some of his historical patterns of behavior, lashing out at his colleagues. While this behavior certainly wasn't well received by his team members, it served as continued learning on how to manage his emotions under the most exacting of situations as well as a reminder that learning is an ongoing process.

Moreover, ripeness varies by task and situation – even within the same individual. A person can be very ripe for change on a certain task, but not another. Differences in incentives drives this, such that one is incented to address one growth area far more than they are to address another. Alternatively, we have worked with people who see some elements of their behavior being more hardwired than others are, and the coachee chooses to address those that seemed to have the best chance to make meaningful adjustments. Ultimately, effective coaches focus their help on those behavioral changes that will make a meaningful difference for the coachee and their organization —often ignoring other possible behavioral changes that are less changeable, less valuable, or less of a priority.

THE MODEL IN SUMMARY

R (Realization): The Light Bulb and the Blame Game

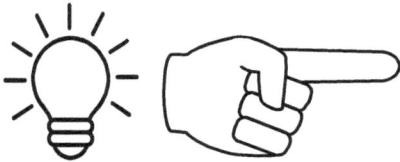

There are two parts to Realization: the personal recognition that there is a need for change, and assuming the personal accountability for making this change. Both parts need to be operative for the realization to fully kick in. The first part, Recognition, is about having a general understanding about the need for something to change. However, this is not sufficient to propel a full realization, as responsibility for that change could be attributed to anyone or anything. For instance, we coached a leader who was aware that she was perceived as being a loose cannon and politically unsavvy. However, this person justified the behavior by saying that she was simply articulating what others thought but wouldn't say aloud. In a sense, she was suggesting that she should be admired for the courageousness of her behavior. Thus, while she acknowledged that a challenge existed, she was, initially, not assuming responsibility for the need to change her behavior. This second element, Ownership, is crucial because it's about taking some level of accountability for the fact that one's behavior may be contributing to the problem.

Furthermore, individuals need to pivot past the passivity and helplessness of the victim response and take personal accountability for resolving the issue at hand. The most gifted coaches invariably excel in promoting this sense of personal accountability. Hopefully, you noticed this theme of personal accountability heavily referenced throughout our parable and got some insights about how to eliminate that blame game and promote more of a "buck stops here" mentality within yourself or those you are coaching.

As the acronym RIPEN indicates, there are multiple aspects toward becoming ripe for a specific change—the more the better—but Realization is the only prerequisite for change. If people don't realize that a change needs to be made and don't assume personal ownership for making such a change, the chances are negligible that they will actually change their behavior.

People come to their own personal realization in many ways. . This realization may come in the form of an insightful "light bulb moment" that a leader gets from 360° feedback, a discussion with his or her manager or coach, a painful failure, or any number of sources. Effective coaches help their coachees to come to their realizations by themselves, instead of immediately telling them what they should realize. Attempt to use thought-provoking questions and feedback to get the coachee to connect the dots and come to their own realizations—that way the lessons are much more likely to be internalized. An overly direct, one-way approach may not be challenged, but is apt to be met with resistance, preventing the realization from clicking and, therefore, will not support or energize the difficult process of behavior change.

Start by empathizing. Ask questions. Get curious. Understand the issues from their perspective. Then, be direct and provocative when you need to be, while still acknowledging the other's perspective. Sometimes people need to hear feedback in a penetrating way. Individuals have lived within their skin for their entire lifetime and grown accustomed to their behaviors and outcomes. Sometimes a jolting message is necessary to enhance their clarity.

We were reminded of our tendency to portray feedback in a direct and provocative manner by a former coaching client. Feedback we collected on behalf of this individual suggested she was regarded as an up and coming superstar in the organization. However, concerns were voiced regarding her trustworthiness, self-centered motivations, and generally political demeanor. We were fairly direct in our messaging of these issues, and you can imagine the anxiety this caused her. Images of her imploding upward mobility flashed across her mind for a full day after she read the report. When we met to debrief the report, one of her first questions was, "How serious is this feedback?" Years later she reminded us of our provocative response (which we had forgotten about until that point). Specifically, our response to her question was, "Well, it's not necessarily a career killer." The implicit message was it could be a career killer if she didn't do something about it! Not only did this directness promote a high level of Realization that the status quo wasn't working as well as she had thought, but it also heavily hit on her core incentives of wanting to be promoted and have a positive impact on the organization. Unsurprisingly, she made significant changes to her approach, fostering more of a team mentality, and has continued to be very successful.

Many leaders have a blind spot and lack a basic understanding that a problem exists, so the delivery of pointed feedback can come as a wake-up call to them. It can be the switch to turn their "lightbulb" on.

I (Incentive): Gas Pedals and Parking Brakes

Tapping into personally meaningful incentives is critical to promoting openness to change. The single biggest mistake most coaches make is assuming that their own view of incentives is shared by their coachees and therefore sufficiently meaningful to encourage the hard work associated with change. Instead, we believe that great coaches need to take the time to understand what makes the *other* person tick. What are *their* incentives? What are *they* trying to accomplish personally and professionally? What are *they* trying to avoid?

There are the two fundamental incentives for change: *Approach Incentives* - the possibility of gaining certain outcomes ("If I do this, it'll help me get promoted") and *Avoidance Incentives* - the possibility of avoiding certain outcomes ("If I don't do this, my influence will decrease"). Never underestimate the importance of one's personal values when considering personally meaningful incentives to motivate your coachees to make a change. In our parable, Rick's personal values around fairness and teamwork play a significant role in him adopting a different approach with Ivan. Money or aspirations towards a promotion weren't needed to get him to shift his behavior. Instead, Rick didn't want to be a hypocrite and acted out of accordance with his personal values.

Regardless of whether the incentive is internal (Rick's personal values around fairness and teamwork) or external (Ivan realizing that if he didn't behave more collaboratively, the meeting with Ten Zero could be a disaster), incentives serve as the "gas pedal" to getting things moving and an individual motivated to start changing key behaviors.

However, savvy coaches know that counter-incentives are often at play and prevent people from changing. These often serve as the "parking brakes" on a car. When people aren't changing their ways, chances are high that it's for a reason. The status quo is working for them in some way that needs to be understood and explored. Whatever the situation, it's always worth examining not just what incentives a person has to change, but what counter-incentives she or he has to *not* make a change. Fear of the unknown, risk of failure, and complacency are common examples of counter-incentives. Explicitly probing into why someone *wouldn't* want to change what they are doing is a great way to start to understand the counter-incentives that may be working against change.

P (Pressure): The Ticking Clock

Pressure is associated with the perceived urgency of making specific changes. Think of pressure as a ticking clock, counting down the remaining time one perceives to make a certain change. As a manager or leader, if you're wondering if your people are feeling sufficient pressure, ask yourself, "Do they believe making this change can wait until next week? Next month? Next quarter?" If the answer is, "Yes," then they may not feel sufficient urgency to make the changes you want. Without pressure, things languish in the "important but not urgent" bucket. We probably all have some example of a change we want to make that has been on our "to-do" list for years, whether its personal improvement or professional development, but have failed to take action on. It's probably not because we think its unimportant, but because we haven't yet come to the conclusion that it has to happen immediately "or else".

Pressure can take many forms: a big client opportunity, a large organizational change, a new boss, a newly announced opening, or an opportunity to interact with C-suite executives. Regardless of the form pressure takes, it can be just the thing needed to prompt someone to kick their development into gear. If they don't feel like the change must happen immediately, the chance of starting the behavior change decreases, as do the chances that they will stick with early adjustments if they don't payoff right away. Some behavior changes that you would like to see in the people you coach can certainly wait a few weeks or a few months and therefore pressure is unimportant, but for the changes that can't be delayed, people must feel the increasing pressure required to drive action *now*, not later.

E (Expectation): The Help Hotline

If Realization, Incentive and Pressure are factors impacting people's motivation for change, Expectation impacts people's belief that they can actually make that change. It affects how hopeful and confident they are.

As we indicated previously, Expectation is our layman's label for the academic concept, "self-efficacy," or a person's belief in their ability to achieve a certain goal. Expectation relates both to an individual's confidence in their ability to accomplish a task, as well as their actual ability to accomplish the task. Psychologist Albert Bandura, the pioneer of this concept, explains that people with high self-efficacy or a high level of expectation are more likely to view difficult tasks as something to be mastered than something to be avoided. Expectation relates to one's confidence in his or her ability to accomplish a task. Individuals with high levels of expectation are more motivated and resilient when facing obstacles than their lower expectation counterparts.

We raise expectation by mapping out a path of change, and equipping people with experiences, tips, resources and role models to help them make the change in addition to generally building their confidence through motivating and 'safety-netting'.

In some ways, this element of the model is the most natural component. Managers are drawn to raising expectation – through either telling people how to do something, or cheerleading them on the way to do something. This is often what most managers and coaches tend to default towards first when coaching others. This is certainly an important step, but the best time to get into expectation building is not right away, but when people explicitly ask for it.

Timing of expectation building is critical. Only when Stephan asked Rick, "So what is the right question to ask Nytasha?" was Stephan truly ready to hear Rick's advice. Similarly, only when Ivan asked Rick for his opinion on what to do to encourage more debate and not shut down discussions was he going to listen to what Rick had to say. From our experience, all the other factors of our model – Realization, Incentive, Pressure – ought to be lined up in some way before managers get into the nitty-gritty of building skill and motivation. If Realization, Incentive, and Pressure aren't sufficiently high, advice either goes in one ear and out the other, or it creates compliance oriented behavior (I have to read this article because my boss sent it to me) rather than becoming a learning experience.

Another best practice regarding building expectation is to ensure people feel a sense of accomplishment and mastery on the issue they're working on. Giving them positive feedback or reminding them of how they've done something similar in the past helps raise people's expectation. Managers tend to be too stingy when it comes to utilizing positive feedback to reinforce behavior change efforts. We have come to believe that managers don't utilize positive feedback sufficiently when coaching because they don't want the coachee, who is, in their eyes, only halfway to adopting the new behavior, to think that they are done. In other words, they don't want to convey a mixed message about their standards. However, to the coachee, halfway there is a pretty darn good effort, and many of them would like their bosses to provide some recognition, which will sustain their behavior change efforts.

Furthermore, one can mitigate the risk of mixed messages around standards by highlighting recognition for the progress that has been made, then subsequently identifying what even better looks like. For example, a manager might highlight that they notice that their direct report has been making an effort to listen to others more effectively, citing specific examples of this and discussing the impact this listening is having on others, and then identifying instances when the individual's listening continues to be poor.

We saw this exact scenario recently, during a discussion with a CEO about development efforts with his executive team. He mentioned that one of his team members "hadn't really made much progress" on his goal to be more collaborative and work well across the organization. But, when pushed on this perspective, he acknowledged that the leader, in fact, had made incremental progress. The CEO didn't want to "give him credit for something so minor and cause him to ease up on his effort."

We see this mentality all the time – managers and coaches not wanting to ease up on the pressure to make further change – but as long as you are very clear about both progress-to-date and the need for further improvement, you are capturing the value of reinforcement with the clarity needed to push more change.

N (Natural Inclination): Headwinds and Tailwinds

There is a spectrum of Natural Inclination. On one end of it, people with low natural inclination (who may be very successful due to having some outstanding skills) believe their abilities are fixed assets or deficits. They believe that their success naturally comes to them and are unable to veer outside of their comfort zone. People with low natural inclination are not likely to seek out feedback or stretch assignments that demand the development of new skills. They don't believe they are capable of deep change.

You can think of having low natural inclination as having a headwind – it will make the development journey more difficult, but not impossible. In these situations the other elements of the model (particularly incentive) need to be emphasized. Having high natural inclination, on the other hand, acts as a tailwind, accelerating and speeding the journey of change. Instead of a "fixed mindset," those high in natural inclination have a "growth mindset." People with a growth mindset believe that their most basic abilities can be developed through curiosity, dedication, and hard work. In other words, while natural talent matters to them, they believe it is just a starting point.

People with high natural inclination are generally committed to self-improvement, and open to new experiences and learning new things or skills.

As a coach, it can be nice to work with someone who is naturally inclined to be open and willing to be stretched and challenged, but that doesn't automatically mean they are high on every other dimension of the model. Be sure to check that they have the Realization, Incentive, Pressure, and Expectation – on the specific issue they need to change – before you get too confident about the fact that they are generally open to change and adapt.

CONCLUSION

We have introduced the RIPEN framework to you as a way of thinking about coaching and individual behavior change. However, as we hint at in Betsy and Rick's conversations about getting the workforce ready for change, one can certainly apply the principles of our RIPEN model more broadly to organizational change management. In the case of Karpos, the issue was that the workforce was high on Pressure and Realization, but low on Expectation, or the confidence that they could pull off the changes required of them. Betsy had drilled into people the need for a shift in business strategy and the urgency around declining profits, but she hadn't provided sufficient training and encouragement or properly equipped them to help the workforce become more service-oriented and customer-centric. That, coupled with her harsh demeanor, lowered people's expectation and confidence that they could pull off the changes required.

So, although much of this book is focused on individual, one-on-one coaching relationships, the RIPEN concepts can be expanded for larger organizational units. It can also be very useful in one's own personal life!

In an ever and rapidly changing world, whether in business or personal dynamics, the RIPEN model can be applied for continuous improvement and development.

Sacha Lindekens, Ph.D.

Sacha Lindekens is a Partner with Avion Consulting. He specializes in executive coaching, high potential development and designing and delivering leadership development programs for organizations ranging from large multinational organizations to small to mid-sized family owned entities. His client base is a principally, but not exclusively, in the professional services, financial services, technology/media, and health-care industries. Sacha is a published author in Forbes and T+D on the topic of executive coaching and leadership development. He is also a co-author of the recently released book *How Leaders Improve: A Playbook for Leaders Who Want to Get Better Now,* an Amazon.com #1 new release.

Sacha has a particular interest in assisting leaders to deploy emotionally intelligent leadership. He consults with organizations to create robust leadership pipelines; attract, develop and retain high potentials; and enable executive teams to operate at their full potential. As a coach, he is known for his tendency of being supportive yet direct.

Prior to joining Avion Consulting as an owner in January 2015, Sacha worked at Leadership Research Institute as a consultant for 13 years. Prior to this, Sacha was trained as a psychologist. He worked as a therapist, taught a variety of university level courses, and assisted an NFL team in conducting psychological profiles on incoming rookies to determine their draftability and fit with the organization. Sacha has led teams of consultants and researchers for 20 years. His leadership balances results with strong working relationships. Sacha holds a Ph.D. in Counseling Psychology from the University of Florida, an M.Ed. in Counseling Psychology from Rutgers University and a B.A. in Psychology from SUNY Albany. He was a recipient of the CLAS Fellowship at the University of Florida. He is certified in the use of a wide array of psychometric assessments.

Sacha and his wife live in Carlsbad, CA with their 2 daughters. He enjoys a wide range of outdoor activities including surfing, gardening, barbequing, hiking, mountain biking and golfing.

Jeff Graddy, Ph.D.

Jeff Graddy is a Partner with Avion Consulting, a firm specializing in leadership, team, and organizational development. Jeff's passion is helping leaders get the best out of themselves and their people. He coaches senior executives and high potential talent in order to maximize their impact on the business by focusing on their impact on people. Jeff also helps organizations create innovative leadership development programs, specifically targeting the growth of future leaders who need to possess the emotional intelligence, personal agility, and influencing skills necessary to lead effectively in an increasingly dynamic, connected, global context.

Jeff is honored to advise premier organizations, including market leaders in healthcare, financial services, automotive, retail, technology, professional services, private equity, pharma, and not-for-profit. He takes pride in the long-term nature of his client relationships and the high impact achieved through those partnerships over the last 15 years as a leadership advisor.

Before his organizational consulting career, Jeff was in private practice as a sport psychology consultant, working with elite athletes and teams to help them leverage psychological principles for better performance. Jeff originally started his career in behavioral healthcare, serving both private and government sectors. He held roles that ranged in focus from community mental health care to leading crisis response teams.

Jeff holds a Ph.D. in Counseling Psychology from the University of Florida, where he also earned a Master's degree in Sport Psychology. He completed his doctoral residency at the University of San Diego.

Jeff lives in Estero, Florida with his wife and two children. He sits on the Board of the SWFL Children's Advocacy Center, and is also an Advisory Board member of the Golisano Children's Hospital of Southwest Florida. In his free time, Jeff loves offshore fishing, adventure travel, hacking his way around the golf course, and trying to stay upright on his paddleboard.

www.ingramcontent.com/pod-product-compliance
Lightning Source LLC
Chambersburg PA
CBHW030842210326
41521CB00025B/636